THE PERSONNEL EVALUATION STANDARDS

THE JOINT COMMITTEE ON STANDARDS
FOR EDUCATIONAL EVALUATION

Daniel L. Stufflebeam
Chair

THE PERSONNEL EVALUATION STANDARDS

How to Assess Systems for Evaluating Educators

Sponsored by

American Association of School Administrators
American Association of School Personnel Administration
American Educational Research Association
American Evaluation Association
American Federation of Teachers
American Psychological Association
Association for Measurement and Evaluation in Counseling
    and Development
Association for Supervision and Curriculum Development
Education Commission of the States
National Association of Elementary School Principals
National Association of Secondary School Principals
National Council on Measurement in Education
National Education Association
National School Boards Association

SAGE PUBLICATIONS
The International Professional Publishers
Newbury Park   London   New Delhi

For information address:

SAGE Publications, Inc.
2455 Teller Road
Newbury Park, California 91320

SAGE Publications Ltd.
6 Bonhill Street
London EC2A 4PU
United Kingdom

SAGE Publications India Pvt. Ltd.
M-32 Market
Greater Kailash I
New Delhi 110 048 India

Library of Congress Cataloging-in-Publication Data

Main entry under title:

Joint Committee on Standards for Educational Evaluation.
    The personnel evaluation standards : how to assess systems for evaluating educators / [developed by] the Joint Committee on Standards for Educational Evaluation.
        p.   cm.
    Bibliography: p.
    Includes indexes.
    ISBN 0-8039-3360-6   ISBN 0-8039-3361-4 (pbk.)
    1. School personnel management—United States. 2. Education-
-Standards—United States—Evaluation.   I. Title.
LB2831.5.J65   1988
371.1'44—dc19   88-18189
                                                                         CIP
THIRD PRINTING, 1991

Book designed by Sidney Solomon

THE JOINT COMMITTEE

Chair

Daniel L. Stufflebeam (Western Michigan University)

Committee Members

James Adams (Indianapolis Public Schools), representing the American Association of School Administrators

Ralph Alexander (University of Akron), representing the American Psychological Association

Marvin C. Alkin (UCLA), representing the American Educational Research Association (1987-)

Beverly Anderson (Education Commission of the States), representing the Education Commission of the States

Esther Diamond (Educational and Psychological Consultant), representing the Association for Measurement and Evaluation in Counseling and Development

A. Keith Esch (Wichita Public Schools), representing the American Association of School Personnel Administrators

Ronald K. Hambleton (University of Massachusetts), representing the National Council on Measurement in Education

Philip L. Hosford (New Mexico State University), representing the Association for Supervision and Curriculum Development

William Mays, Jr. (Michigan Elementary and Middle School Principals Association), representing the National Association of Elementary School Principals

Carol Norman (National Education Association), representing the National Education Association (1985)

Diana Pullin (Boston College), member-at-large

Marilyn Rauth (American Federation of Teachers), representing the American Federation of Teachers

James R. Sanders (Western Michigan University), representing the American Evaluation Association

Sheila Simmons-Merrick (National Education Association), representing the National Education Association (1986-)

Scott D. Thomson (National Association of Secondary School Principals), representing the National Association of Secondary School Principals

JoAnn Wimmer (National School Boards Association), representing the National School Boards Association

Linda Winfield (Temple University), representing the American Educational Research Association (1984-1986)

CONTENTS

FUNCTIONAL TABLE OF CONTENTS

Defining a Role

Most applicable standards:

Selection

Most applicable standards:

Performance Reviews

Most applicable standards:

Counseling for Staff Development

Most applicable standards:

Merit Awards

Most applicable standards:

Termination
Most applicable standards:

ACKNOWLEDGMENTS

The development of this document was supported by grants from the Besser Foundation, the Exxon Education Foundation, the Lilly Endowment, Inc., the Conrad N. Hilton Foundation, and the Western Michigan University Foundation. Additional support was provided by the organizations that appointed the members of the Joint Committee: American Association of School Administrators, American Association of School Personnel Administrators, American Educational Research Association, American Evaluation Association, American Federation of Teachers, American Psychological Association, Association for Measurement and Evaluation in Counseling and Development, Association for Supervision and Curriculum Development, Education Commission of the States, National Association of Elementary School Principals, National Association of Secondary School Principals, National Council on Measurement in Education, National Education Association, and National School Boards Association. Many persons assisted the Joint Committee in developing this document; the members of the various support groups are listed in Appendix C. The Joint Committee thanks those organizations and individuals who helped in developing this document. However, the Joint Committee is solely responsible for the contents of this document. The formal endorsement of the sponsoring groups has not been sought or given.

> Royalties from the sales of the published version of this document will be used to promote effective use of *The Personnel Evaluation Standards* and to support ongoing review and revision activities.

INVITATION TO USERS

The Personnel Evaluation Standards is the product of a collaborative effort to present educational institutions with criteria and guidelines for assessing and improving their systems for evaluating the qualifications and performances of educators. The contents have undergone extensive review and refinement. Nevertheless, the standards are subject to further examination, revision, and expansion. To ensure that future revisions of *The Personnel Evaluation Standards* build on the experience and insight of users, the Joint Committee invites those who use the standards to submit their criticisms, observations, and recommendations. To help in this process, the Committee has prepared a package of information consisting of a letter of acknowledgment, information about the review and revision process, and a supply of feedback forms with directions for their use. These forms request that the user:

a. Describe roles and responsibilities—e.g., those of the evaluators, evaluatees, and other audiences—of persons or groups involved in the evaluation system being examined.

b. Summarize the evaluation system in relation to each standard.

c. Provide copies of pertinent evaluation instruments and report formats used in the system.

d. Note any problems in applying individual standards, as well as conflicts among standards.

e. Describe how any such conflicts were resolved.

f. Identify limitations in individual standards and offer recommendations for refinement or revision.

g. Identify areas not covered by the standards.

The Joint Committee has also developed a citation form, shown in Appendix B, that the user of *The Personnel Evaluation Standards* may wish to attach to evaluation plans, contracts, reports, and the like to which *The Personnel Evaluation Standards* have been applied.

Address all inquiries to:

> The Joint Committee on Standards for
>   Educational Evaluation
> The Evaluation Center
> Western Michigan University
> Kalamazoo, MI 49008-5178

INTRODUCTION

This book is a guide for assessing or developing systems for evaluating education personnel. It presents and elaborates 21 standards by which to plan and assess systems for evaluating teachers, professors, administrators, counselors, and other educators. It is intended to be used (along with other materials) by board members and educators in school districts, colleges, universities, state education departments, accrediting agencies, and other educational institutions. Basically, the standards require that evaluations be proper, useful, feasible, and accurate.

The standards were developed by a Joint Committee with representatives from fourteen major professional associations concerned with education. The Joint Committee recommends that educational institutions adopt this book as their primary reference for developing, assessing, upgrading, and implementing institutional policies and procedures for evaluating education personnel.

The Need for Personnel Evaluation in Education

The need for sound evaluation of education personnel is clear. In order to educate students effectively and to achieve other related goals, educational institutions must use evaluation to select, retain, and develop qualified personnel and to manage and facilitate their work.

This need has a number of important dimensions. Colleges of education and state education departments should carefully evaluate entry-level educators before certifying or licensing them to teach or advise students or to administer schools. To guide hiring decisions, faculty committees, administrators, and policy boards should conduct rigorous evaluations to identify promising job candidates and assess their qualifications to carry out particular assignments. Following hiring decisions, peer review committees, administrators, and board members should periodically assess the performance of individual educators for a host of key purposes: guiding promotion and tenure decisions, recognizing and rewarding meritorious contributions, helping faculty and administrators take stock of their strengths, helping them discover where they need improvement, prescribing remediation goals and activities, and, when remediation efforts fail, developing a fair, valid, and effective case for terminating those who are harmful to students or otherwise ineffective. Administrators and faculty committees also need feedback from performance reviews and other needs assessment data in order to plan meaningful staff development activities. Clearly, the need for personnel evaluations in educational institutions is pervasive, important, and multifaceted.

The Failure of Personnel Evaluation in Education

However, despite its centrality, educational institutions have often been ineffective in carrying out their personnel evaluation responsibilities. Their failure is documented in many recent reports and books that call for reforms in the evaluation of education personnel (Andrews, 1985; Blumberg, 1980; Boyer, 1983; Brodinsky, 1984; *Carnegie Task Force on Teaching as a Profession,* 1986; Coker, Medley, & Soar, 1980; Davis & Arnof, 1983; *Educating Americans for the 21st Century*—National Science Foundation, 1983; Goodlad, 1983; *Making the Grade*—Peterson, 1983; Millman, 1981; *A Nation at Risk*—National Commission on Excellence in Education, 1983; Soar, Medley, & Coker, 1983; Wise & Darling-Hammond, 1985.) The deficiencies of education personnel evaluation—and their cost—are also reflected in numerous court cases. (For example, see Andrews, 1985; Johnson, 1982; Rood, 1977; Strike & Bull, 1981). Testimony presented at public hearings on an earlier draft of this book was replete with charges, and examples, that personnel evaluations repeatedly have been invalid, unfair, superficial, and ineffective. (Problems in education personnel evaluation and the need for standards are elaborated in Appendix A.)

Overall, dominant criticisms of education personnel evaluation practices are that they have failed to:

— Screen out unqualified persons from certification and selection processes
— Provide constructive feedback to individual educators
— Recognize and help reinforce outstanding service

— Provide direction for staff development programs

— Provide evidence that will withstand professional and judicial scrutiny

— Provide evidence efficiently and at reasonable cost

— Aid institutions in terminating incompetent or unproductive personnel

— Unify, rather than divide, teachers and administrators in their collective efforts to educate students

The Functions of the Standards

The function of these standards is to correct deficiencies in current practice and present educators and policy board members with a widely shared view of general principles for developing and assessing sound, acceptable personnel evaluation procedures and with practical advice for implementing them.

Development of the Standards

The sixteen-member Joint Committee coordinated the project and co-authored *The Personnel Evaluation Standards*. The Committee studied personnel evaluation practices and obtained input from hundreds of teachers, administrators, board members, and others involved with the evaluation of education personnel. A national Panel of Writers helped to write the first draft of *The Personnel Evaluation Standards*. National and international Review Panels critiqued that draft, which the Joint Committee, aided by their responses, then rewrote. Some forty knowledgeable professionals critiqued the second draft in public hearings, and that draft was also field tested in various institutional settings throughout the United States. A Validation Panel monitored and evaluated the overall project. The Joint Committee considered all of that feedback in creating this book. (A detailed description of the project's participants and process is provided in Appendix A.)

Definitions

The Committee defines personnel evaluation as *the systematic assessment of a person's performance and/or qualifications in relation to a professional role and some specified and defensible institutional purpose.* It defines a standard as "a principle commonly agreed to by people engaged in the professional practice of evaluation for the measurement of the value or the quality of an evaluation" (Joint Committee, 1981, p. 12).

Guiding Assumptions

Five major assumptions have guided the Committee's work.

First, the fundamental purpose of personnel evaluation or any other education activity must be to provide effective services to students and society. This book is dedicated to the proposition that personnel evaluation can and must be designed and conducted to encourage and guide educators to serve all students more effectively and to advance the theory and practice of education.

Second, personnel evaluation practices should be constructive and free of unnecessarily threatening or demoralizing characteristics. When individuals have confidence in the evaluation criteria and process, when they experience clear communication and fair treatment, and when they see evaluation contributing to their success, they are more likely to be enthusiastic in their work and receptive to evaluation.

Third, personnel evaluations are vital for planning sound professional development experiences. It is, for example, demeaning and wasteful to ask or require all staff members to take particular courses or training when some already possess the necessary knowledge and skills. Evaluation should point the way to new learning for individuals that is directly related to their needs, interests, and responsibilities.

Fourth, disagreements about what constitutes good teaching, good administration, and good research may complicate personnel evaluation, but such disagreements are warranted. Job descriptions and educational approaches vary legitimately because of different philosophies of education, different state or institutional policies, different local needs and orientations, and different institutional goals, among other reasons. In addition, the education establishment does not agree about what conditions, qualifications, and performances are necessary and sufficient for achieving given educational objectives. Depending upon the circumstances, a variety of approaches may be more or less effective in different situations. For these reasons, the Joint Committee has adopted a pluralistic view regarding application of these standards. Users of the standards must define their own educational goals, approaches, and role definitions, and then apply the standards accordingly.

Fifth, personnel evaluations vary in complexity and importance; consequently, applications of the standards may be crucial in some circumstances but out of place or even counterproductive in others. When a personnel decision is in doubt and might have to be defended in court, prudence dictates a thorough and well-documented evaluation. When it is clear, however, that a positive judgment is appropriate and desirable, the institution should act accordingly. In general, more time and effort should be devoted to applying standards when personnel actions are doubtful or potentially controversial. In those cases, the standards can contribute most by promoting sound evaluations and by assuring all interested parties of the rationality, fairness, and defensibility of the decisions.

Points of Clarification

Some words of caution are appropriate.

First, the standards present criteria for judging evaluation plans, procedures, and reports. The book is **not** an attempt to define good teaching, good administration, good counseling, or any other educational role.

Second, the standards were developed for use in the United States. They might or might not apply in other national settings. The constituents for this book are the sponsoring organizations, and the vast majority of their members are involved in U.S. education institutions. In order to serve these constituents, we have described principles that undergird U.S. ideals, laws, and education systems and have used examples that are familiar in the United States. We appreciate the useful reviews and suggestions from international colleagues, and we intend to contribute to continued international exchange in education personnel evaluation. However, we have **not** tried to develop standards that fit the laws, systems, and circumstances of other countries.

Domain of the Standards

The standards focus on systems used to evaluate the performance and qualifications of individuals. Moreover, they are intended to apply to a broad range of existing techniques (including observation, interview, applied performance tests, licensure tests, professional skills tests, development of a portfolio, supervisor assessment, peer assessment, and student assessment) and to new evaluation approaches as they are developed.

The standards are for use in schools, postsecondary institutions, and other agencies whose primary function is to educate. They are aimed at all professional jobs with responsibility for student growth and development. Such jobs include teaching, advising, and counseling students; supporting instruction and developing curricula; administering schools and colleges and developing education policy; and conducting education research.

The standards apply to systems used for all types of education personnel evaluation. These include evaluation practices for determining entry into professional training; certifying competence; granting a license to practice; defining a role; selecting from a pool of job applicants; monitoring and providing feedback about performance; counseling for staff development; determining merit awards; and deciding about tenure, promotion, recertification, and dismissal. In general, they apply to all questions clearly related to the job of the professional educator, including the educator's qualifications, performance, effectiveness, and relationships with other educators.

Nature of the Standards

The standards are presented at the level of elaborated general principles. Thus, for example, while it is essential to measure personnel performance reliably, no criterion level is defined that differentiates sharply between acceptable and unacceptable reliability. Given the state of the art, to do so would be indefensible. Such oversimplification would inappropriately emphasize the labeling of evaluations as sound or unsound without providing direction for improving them; general principles suffice for the latter purpose, while leaving room for creative and locally responsive evaluation procedures.

Each standard provides a summary description of the principle involved, a discussion of its key concepts and importance, guidelines for carrying it out, common mistakes to be avoided, and one or more illustrations of how the standard aplies in particular evaluative situations. The standards are presented in a common format to make them easier to relate and use. (See Figure 1.)

Substance of the Standards

The 21 standards are divided into four general categories that correspond to four basic attributes of sound evaluation: propriety, utility, feasibility, and accuracy.

Propriety Standards

The five Propriety Standards reflect the fact that personnel evaluations may violate or fail to address certain ethical and legal principles. The primary principle is that schools exist to serve students; therefore, personnel evaluations should concentrate on determining whether educators are effectively meeting the needs of students. In general, the Propriety Standards are aimed at protecting the rights of persons affected by an evaluation, including students, instructors, counselors, administrators, and evaluators. The topics of these standards are Service Orientation, Formal Evaluation Guidelines, Conflict of Interest, Access to Personnel Evaluation Reports, and Interaction with Evaluatees. Overall, the Propriety Standards require that evaluations be conducted legally, ethically, and with due regard for the welfare of students, other clients, and educators.

Utility Standards

The five Utility Standards are intended to guide evaluations so that they will be informative, timely, and influential. Especially, these standards require that evaluations provide information useful to individuals and to groups of educators in improving

FIGURE 1
Components of a Standard

Descriptor:	For example, Service Orientation
Standard:	A definition of the standard in the form of a "should" statement; i.e., the Service Orientation standard is stated as follows: "Evaluations of educators should promote sound education principles, fulfillment of institutional missions, and effective performance of job responsibilities, so that the educational needs of students, community, and society are met."
Explanation:	A conceptual introductory statement that defines key terms in the standard and describes the essence of the requirements embodied in the standard.
Rationale:	A generalized argument for the inclusion of the standard.
Guidelines:	A list of procedural suggestions intended to help evaluators and their audiences to meet the requirements of the evaluation standard. These are strategies to avoid mistakes in applying the standard. The guidelines should not be considered exhaustive or mandatory. Rather, they are procedures to consider and to follow when the evaluator judges them to be potentially helpful and feasible.
Common Errors:	Warnings about typical problems in conducting personnel evaluations, as well as possible negative side effects resulting from taking one standard too seriously without considering its impact on other standards.
Illustrative Case:	One or more illustrations. These show how the standard might be applied, including the description of a certain setting, a situation in which the standard is not met, an analysis of the attending problems, and a discussion of corrective actions that would result in meeting the standard. The corrective actions discussed are only illustrative and are not intended to encompass all possible corrections. As much as possible, the illustrative cases have been based on actual evaluations. Also, each case is slanted directly to highlight the salient points in the particular standard, rather than to encompass points across all of the standards.
Supporting Documentation:	Selected references listed at the end of each standard to assist the reader in further study in the general realm of the standard.

their performance. The Utility Standards also require that evaluations be focused on predetermined uses, such as informing selection and tenure decisions or providing direction for staff development, and that they be conducted by persons with appropriate expertise and credibility. The topics of the Utility Standards are Constructive Orientation, Defined Uses, Evaluator Credibility, Functional Reporting, and Follow-Up and Impact. In general, these standards view personnel evaluation as an integral part of an institution's ongoing effort to recruit outstanding staff members, and, through timely and relevant evaluative feedback, to encourage and guide them to deliver high quality service.

Feasibility Standards

The three Feasibility Standards promote evaluations that are efficient, easy to use, viable in the face of social, political, and governmental forces and constraints, and that will be adequately funded. The topics of these standards are Practical Procedures, Political Viability, and Fiscal Viability.

Accuracy Standards

The eight Accuracy Standards aim at determining whether an evaluation has produced sound information about an educator's qualifications or performance. The topics are Defined Role, Work Environment, Documentation of Procedures, Valid Measurement, Reliable Measurement, Systematic Data Control, Bias Control, and Monitoring Evaluation Systems. The overall rating of a personnel evaluation against the Accuracy Standards gives a good assessment of the evaluation's validity.

Uses of the Standards

These standards are intended primarily to help four main groups to implement their evaluation responsibilities.

The first group includes the prime audiences for personnel evaluations: educational administrators, faculty committees, members of policy boards, and others. They can use the standards as follows:

1. To provide the primary reference document for developing and applying board policy on personnel evaluation

2. To foster due process in evaluation practices, thereby providing fair treatment and reducing legal vulnerability in personnel evaluation cases

3. To assess and improve institutional evaluation systems used in certification, selection, assignment, reassignment, promotion, tenure, and other types of recognition and decisions

4. To strengthen the role of personnel evaluation in ensuring high standards of teaching, administration, research, and service

5. To help assure that new policy initiatives—e.g., incentive pay, career ladders, and mentoring programs—can accomplish their objectives and are appropriately assessed

6. To help clarify the rights and responsibilities of professionals in the institution

7. To help assure that personnel evaluations hold educators accountable for delivery of high quality services

8. To promote evaluation practices that help the institution attract, develop, and retain qualified educators

9. To promote evaluations that reinforce positive behaviors, as well as identify areas for improvement, and thereby foster greater job satisfaction and performance

10. To obtain evaluations that provide a just and defensible basis for terminating educators who persist in providing unacceptable services

The second audience for these standards includes principals, deans, department chairs, faculty, and others when they are serving in the role of personnel evaluator. They can use the standards:

1. To train those who are to serve in the role of personnel evaluator

2. To examine alternative evaluation approaches and systems

3. To plan particular evaluations and overall evaluation systems

4. To guide and monitor particular evaluations

5. To assess particular evaluations

6. To help avoid or settle disputes in the evaluation of personnel

7. To provide direction for addressing specific issues in given evaluations

The third audience for these standards includes teachers, professors, counselors, administrators, and other educators when they are being evaluated. They can use the standards as follows:

1. To improve their understandings of and skills in personnel evaluation
2. To promote or demand evaluations that lead to increased professional development for themselves and other educators
3. To identify and resolve possible due process issues before mistakes occur in an evaluation
4. To investigate whether given personnel evaluations are fair, valid, practical, and educationally useful

The fourth audience for the standards includes those who use *The Personnel Evaluation Standards* for research, development, or teaching. They can use the standards:

1. As a textbook for courses on personnel evaluation or personnel administration
2. As criteria against which to evaluate alternative models for personnel evaluation
3. As a framework for use in developing evaluation systems and better models for personnel evaluation
4. As a logical structure for deriving and investigating questions and hypotheses about personnel evaluation

Tradeoffs Among the Standards

The relative importance of the 21 standards will differ depending upon the type of personnel actions contemplated. Such types include entering into training (admissions), certification and licensing; position analysis; selection; performance review; counseling for staff development; merit or incentive awards; and tenure, promotion, and termination decisions. The evaluations appropriate to these different actions might vary widely in procedures used, timing of data collection, and amount of time and resources invested. Even though all of the standards may be relevant to all personnel decisions, different standards might warrant more or less emphasis depending upon the particular personnel action. Moreover, excessive emphasis on one standard can weaken performance on another; judgment is required when considering how much emphasis to place on each standard. It must be defensible in the context of the particular situation. To help readers address this issue, a summary of the Joint Committee's judgments about which standards are to be weighted most heavily in given personnel actions is presented in Table 1. This table is reflective of the Functional Table of Contents at the front of the book.

Future Development of the Standards

These standards are the product of a comprehensive effort to agree on what constitutes sound systems for personnel evaluation in education. The users of the standards should be alert to problems, especially those unique to specific contexts. The Joint Committee invites users to submit criticisms and recommendations for consideration in the next developmental cycle. The Committee is committed to a five-year review process wherein necessary revision will be made in *The Personnel Evaluation Standards*. Comments and suggestions should be sent to:

> Joint Committee on Standards for
> Educational Evaluation
> The Evaluation Center
> Western Michigan University
> Kalamazoo, MI 49008-5178

Organization of the Book

The remainder of this book is divided into two main parts. Part 1 is a straightforward presentation of the 21 standards. Part 2 presents and illustrates an approach for applying the standards. Appendixes describe the development of the standards, the steps and forms for citing them, a listing of the participants in the development of the standards, a glossary of relevant terms, the bibliography, indexes to the roles, institutions, purposes, and personnel actions addressed in the illustrative cases, and a subject matter index.

Table 1
Joint Committee Median Ratings of Each Standard's Applicability to Evaluations Related to Given Personnel Actions

Evaluations for:

	Entry to Training	Certification/ Licensing	Defining a Role	Selection	Staff Develop-ment	Professional Feed-back & Account-ability	Merit Awards	Tenure Decisions	Promotion Decisions	Termina-tion
Propriety Standards										
P1 Service Orientation	hi	hi	hi	hi	hi	med	med	hi	med	hi
2 Formal Evaluation Guidelines	hi	hi	med	hi	hi	hi	hi	hi	hi	hi
3 Conflict of Interest	hi	hi	lo	hi	med	hi	hi	hi	hi	hi
4 Access to Personnel Evaluation Reports	hi	med	lo	hi	med	hi	med	hi	hi	hi
5 Interactions with Evaluatees	hi	med	med	hi	hi	hi	hi	hi	hi	hi
Utility Standards										
U1 Constructive Orientation	hi	lo	hi	med	hi	hi	hi	med	med	med
2 Defined Uses	hi	hi	lo	med	hi	hi	med	hi	hi	hi
3 Evaluator Credibility	hi	hi	hi	hi	hi	hi	hi	hi	hi	hi
4 Functional Reporting	hi	hi	hi	hi	hi	hi	med	hi	hi	hi
5 Follow-up and Impact	lo	lo	hi	med	hi	hi	med	hi	hi	med
Feasibility Standards										
F1 Practical Procedures	hi	med	hi	hi	hi	med	hi	med	med	med
2 Political Viability	med	hi	hi	hi	med	med	hi	med	med	hi
3 Fiscal Viability	med	med	med	hi	hi	hi	hi	hi	hi	hi
Accuracy Standards										
A1 Defined Role	med	hi	hi	hi	hi	hi	hi	hi	hi	hi
2 Work Environment	lo	lo	hi	hi	hi	hi	med	hi	hi	hi
3 Documentation of Procedures	hi	hi	med	hi	med	hi	hi	hi	hi	hi
4 Valid Measurement	hi	hi	med	hi	hi	med	hi	hi	hi	hi
5 Reliable Measurement	hi	hi	med	hi	hi	med	med	hi	hi	hi
6 Systematic Data Control	hi	hi	med	hi	hi	hi	hi	hi	hi	hi
7 Bias Control	hi	hi	med	hi	hi	hi	hi	hi	hi	hi
8 Monitoring Evaluation Systems	hi	hi	hi	hi	hi	hi	hi	hi	hi	hi

Our Charge to the Users of These Standards

Evaluation of personnel is an essential means of assuring quality in education. Despite that central importance, however, possibly no other area of education has such a negative reputation. Too often, evaluations of teachers and administrators have been divisive and counterproductive. This book is the product of a collaborative effort by fourteen professional associations concerned with improving education, whose objective in this instance is to reform the practice of personnel evaluation in education. We believe that objective can be accomplished through defining and clarifying sound and useful practice and stimulating education institutions to implement effective and defensible personnel evaluation.

The Joint Committee urges educators, legislators, government officials, professional associations, school boards, colleges of education, accrediting agencies, and other interested persons and groups to study, to adopt, and to apply the standards. Applications should be in depth and careful, with the ultimate goal of improving the quality and effectiveness of personnel evaluations as a means of helping educators to provide excellent professional services to students and society.

PART 1

The Standards

PROPRIETY STANDARDS

Summary of the Standards

P Propriety Standards   The Propriety Standards require that evaluations be conducted legally, ethically, and with due regard for the welfare of evaluatees and clients of the evaluations.

P1 Service Orientation   Evaluations of educators should promote sound education principles, fulfillment of institutional missions, and effective performance of job responsibilities, so that the educational needs of students, community, and society are met.

P2 Formal Evaluation Guidelines   Guidelines for personnel evaluations should be recorded in statements of policy, negotiated agreements, and/or personnel evaluation manuals, so that evaluations are consistent, equitable, and in accordance with pertinent laws and ethical codes.

P3 Conflict of Interest   Conflicts of interest should be identified and dealt with openly and honestly, so that they do not compromise the evaluation process and results.

P4 Access to Personnel Evaluation Reports   Access to reports of personnel evaluation should be limited to those individuals with a legitimate need to review and use the reports, so that appropriate use of the information is assured.

P5 Interactions with Evaluatees   The evaluation should address evaluatees in a professional, considerate, and courteous manner, so that their self-esteem, motivation, professional reputations, performance, and attitude toward personnel evaluation are enhanced or, at least, not needlessly damaged.

> **STANDARD** Evaluations of educators should promote sound education principles, fulfillment of institutional missions, and effective performance of job responsibilities, so that the educational needs of students, community, and society are met.

Explanation The primary purpose of education personnel evaluation is to guide educators to deliver quality educational services. Evaluations should help assure that the institution's goals are understood and pursued, educators' responsibilities specified, students' needs addressed, promised services delivered, professional capabilities advanced, and incompetent or harmful personnel removed.

Those who design, administer, use, and participate in a personnel evaluation system must look beyond educators' self-interests. The rights of students and the community to sound educational services must be upheld, as must the employment rights of administrators, teachers, professors, and other evaluatees.

Rationale Educational systems exist to meet the needs of students and the community; so all elements of those systems, including personnel evaluation, should be directed toward achieving that purpose.

Guidelines

A. Advocate rights of students and community that should be protected by personnel evaluation, such as the rights to equal educational opportunity and competent instruction.

B. Pursue a unified, collaborative effort by the board, administration, and faculty to promote excellence and eliminate incompetence in education; if there is a faculty or administrator union, provide concrete opportunities for them to participate in the collaborative pursuit of excellence.

C. Inform the institution's staff and constituents that personnel evaluation will be directed to recognize and encourage excellent service, motivate and assist all personnel to improve, and document a just cause for dismissing those who remain incompetent or ineffective.

D. Target evaluation resources to those areas most likely to promote the institution's goals: e.g., classroom instruction, administration, and instructional support.

E. Implement a thorough screening process at the time of hiring, followed by one to three years of thorough evaluation to assure sound decisions on retention of personnel.

F. Set and maintain high standards for granting tenure, making sure that the standards are responsive to the needs of students, community, and society.

G. Subject all educators in the institution to a consistent and procedurally fair process of evaluation that can withstand legal scrutiny and, when justified, lead to advancements or successful terminations. (See P-2.)

H. Include steps in the evaluation process that promote the best interests of the students and community. (See P-2 and A-3.)

I. Develop criteria for personnel evaluation that reflect the needs of the students and community and the duties of educators. (See P-2 and A-1.)

J. Include in personnel policies definitions of the types of evaluation findings likely to lead to termination. (See P-2.)

K. Issue official intermediate warnings citing deficiencies that must be remedied if employment is to continue. (See P-2.)

L. Enforce prescribed standards consistently in the personnel evaluation process; e.g., do not relax the expectations of classroom instruction because a teacher is outstanding in some other role, such as coaching, band directing, or community politics.

M. Periodically inform the public about how personnel evaluation is promoting the best interests of the students and community; e.g., describe and discuss the system at meetings of the school board and the parent-teacher organization. (See A-8.)

Common Errors

A. Failing to employ sound evaluation procedures or to act when evaluations clearly identify personnel who are incompetent or harmful.

B. Being overprotective of, or oblivious to, incompetent or harmful personnel.

C. Neglecting to evaluate personnel after they have been awarded tenure.

D. Seeking to remove a marginal or incompetent staff member before attempting to improve that person's performance.

E. Failing to reinforce excellent performance.

F. Failing to invest adequate resources in the development and implementation of evaluation procedures and in the training of evaluators. (See F-3.)

G. Failure to monitor the effectiveness of the personnel evaluation process in serving students and community. (See A-8.)

H. Failing to keep evaluation criteria and practices current with state-of-the-art information on teaching, learning, and evaluation.

Illustrative Case #1—Description   A new superintendent in a small school district reviewed the performance evaluations of her three elementary school principals and found that one principal had been performing poorly for years. He was notorious for his lack of leadership, coming to work late and leaving early, poor communication with parents, and lack of visibility during most of every school day. Teachers in his school functioned independently, and, consequently, the curriculum in the school lacked order and consistent rationale.

Most parents were aware of the situation and requested that their children be placed in other schools. Complaints to the school board had apparently fallen on deaf ears, since the principal was "a good old boy" who was a friend of several board members.

This principal had been in the school district for over twenty years. Rather than build a case and fire him, each superintendent, including the new one, chose not to make waves, opting for "damage control" by letting teachers cover many of the principal's responsibilities.

The new superintendent eventually assigned the principal to the school in the district where presumably he would do the least harm.

Illustrative Case #1—Analysis   The superintendent and the school board acted selfishly and irresponsibly in this situation, to the detriment of all other parties. The superintendent recognized that the principal was unprofessional and violating students' rights to an education. Her own self-interest in job security won out over the interests of the community and students, especially, through the reassignment, those students most often discriminated against. Obviously, no sound evaluation system was in place prior to the new superintendent's arrival, for which the entire school and community paid. The methods of "damage control," unprincipled and uncritical loyalty to senior employees, and avoidance of controversy at such a cost are unacceptable practices when student welfare and the public good is at stake.

Fair and accurate personnel evaluation, with appropriate actions based on the evaluation results, serve a school superintendent well in building staff morale and credibility with the community. The absence of such a system or its misuse invariably harms all of a school's constituencies.

Illustrative Case #1—Suggestions Evaluation of the principal should have been the basis for developing several action options, including his removal. However, since the principal had not been formally and negatively reviewed in the many preceding years, he could have been given other options, such as (1) a time line and directives for improvement, (2) a plan for early retirement, or (3) an assignment to some other position that the evaluation indicated he should be competent to handle.

Illustrative Case #2—Description A newly hired elementary school principal found herself in the uncomfortable position of being required to respond to parental complaints regarding a tenured teacher on her staff. Parents alleged that the teacher could not maintain appropriate classroom control. They also charged that the teacher did not prepare adequately for subject matter presentations and class discussions.

The principal reviewed the teacher's file, and found detailed evidence of previous similar shortcomings. The principal then confirmed these deficiencies by observing the teacher several times, and informed the school board in writing of her concerns about this teacher's competency.

A directive was issued to the teacher, citing her for incompetent classroom instruction, and giving formal notice to remedy.

It specified deficiencies in her teaching performance, and directed her to overcome them during the ensuing school year, and to develop with the principal an improvement plan to assist in meeting that requirement.

During the following school year, the teacher was observed periodically by the principal and three other faculty members, in accordance with local board policies and the negotiated contract. They evaluated the teacher's performance as unsatisfactory, based on lack of control over students, lack of understanding of subject matter, and confused classroom presentations. The teacher was permitted 64 days of remediation, but made no observable improvement.

The teacher was dismissed, an action upheld by the appropriate court, which noted that the district had provided adequate notice of deficiency as well as the opportunity to correct it and assistance in doing so. The court relied on the classroom observations by the principal and faculty members as evidence of this teacher's fundamental teaching inadequacies.

Illustrative Case #2—Analysis   The principal in this case considered the complaints from parents as worthy of attention. She investigated the situation on her own, checking the teacher's file, and making personal classroom observations. The principal followed district procedure in reporting the teacher's deficiencies to the school board, which then formally notified the teacher of her deficiencies, and provided her with a time period for remediation and improvement.

The rights of the teacher were safeguarded by the district. She was observed on multiple occasions by multiple observers. The standard district procedures were used, and she was given specific written feedback, and time and assistance to improve.

The involvement of the board, the principal, and the faculty evaluators demonstrated the commitment of the entire district to safeguarding the rights of students to appropriate and competent instruction. The painstaking collection of documentation and evidence contributed to the court's upholding dismissal of the tenured teacher.

Illustrative Case #2—Suggestions   Charges of incompetent instruction should be addressed as early as possible. If they are not confirmed and dealt with before the tenure decision, they cannot fairly be part of that crucial judgment. Once tenure is granted, dismissal is difficult. If the district had instituted the above procedure before granting tenure to this individual, they would have kept their options open, and they would have shortened the time that district students were exposed to inadequate instruction. Even if the teacher had passed the tenure review and subsequently come under fire for incompetence, detailed investigation and appropriate actions should have been pursued immediately, since, as this case demonstrates, institutions can dismiss or reassign staff in order to protect the interests of students.

Supporting Documentation

Andrews, H. (1985).
Bolton, D. L. (1973).
Landy, F. J., Barnes-Farell, J., & Cleveland, J. N. (1980).
Landy, F. J., Barnes, J. L., & Murphy, K. R. (1978).
Soar, R. S., Medley, D. M., & Coker, H. (1983).
Strike, K., & Bull, B. (1981).

P-2 *Formal Evaluation Guidelines*

> **STANDARD** Guidelines for personnel evaluations should be recorded and provided to employees in statements of policy, negotiated agreements, and/or personnel evaluation manuals, so that evaluations are consistent, equitable, and in accordance with pertinent laws and ethical codes.

Explanation Formal guidelines are the written statements that define the purpose, procedures, and substance of the evaluation. If the evaluation purposes and procedures cannot be stated in reasonably specific terms, they probably are neither clear nor understood.

Pertinent law includes contractual, administrative, statutory, and constitutional provisions that may vary from one locale or state to another. Whatever the jurisdiction, conformance to rights and the procedures that protect these rights are essential elements of successful implementation of personnel evaluation systems.

Rationale Evaluation must be carried out in a consistent, equitable, and legal manner, regardless of who is evaluating and who is being evaluated. Formal guidelines communicate to all involved parties the policies and procedures of personnel evaluation. Written guidelines provide professionals with an opportunity to review and discuss the purposes of evaluation and to ensure protection of both the institution's and the evaluatee's rights. Protecting these rights can help to minimize the likelihood of litigation in personnel matters and promote trust in and support of the personnel evaluation system.

In general, clearly written purposes, criteria, and procedures outlined in policy statements, collective bargaining contracts, and/or evaluation manuals increase the likelihood that performance expectations will be understood, that a uniform standard of judgment will be applied, that evaluations will be fair, that the evaluation results will be respected and used, and that employees will have confidence in both the evaluations and the organization doing the evaluations. Further, clearly stated and fair purposes and procedures will minimize opportunities for successful legal challenge to evaluations.

Guidelines

A. Require in institutional policies that all employees be subject to systematic evaluation.

B. Develop clearly written guidelines for implementing personnel evaluation policies.

C. Ensure that the guidelines address all of the elements for acceptable evaluations set forth in these standards.

D. Concentrate the guidelines on important job-related issues, and avoid listing rules for trivial aspects of the job or matters unrelated to the requirements for successful job performance.

E. Make the guidelines sufficiently specific to guarantee shared understandings of the purposes, procedures, and substance of evaluation.

F. Identify, in the guidelines, the performance reasonably expected of evaluatees in order to be competent and successful on the job.

G. Require that appropriate weights be assigned to each evaluation criterion explicitly and in advance of evaluation.

H. Involve the board and staff in development and periodic review of the policies and guidelines. (See F-2 and A-8.)

I. Ensure that the guidelines meet all local, state, and federal legal requirements concerning employment decisions, such as the state's teacher certification law or a city's non-discrimination ordinance.

J. Explain the plan of personnel evaluation to all employees at least annually and when changes in evaluation are to be implemented.

K. Assure consistent enforcement of the written evaluation guidelines. (See A-8.).

L. Provide a plan of progressive discipline, such as an oral warning, a written warning, disciplinary layoff, and discharge.

M. Define types of evaluation findings likely to lead to termination.

N. Apply the guidelines with a concern for the human dignity and worth of the persons involved. (See P-5.)

O. Establish, in the guidelines, viable review or reevaluation, problem-solving, and appeals procedures to protect all involved in the evaluation.

P. Establish a process for periodic review and revision of evaluation procedures and guidelines. (See A-8.)

Q. Change evaluation guidelines when evaluation practices are changed, when the guidelines are found to be in conflict with applicable law, or when role definitions change.

Common Errors

A. Writing guidelines that are vague, too broad, or confusing.

B. Applying guidelines unevenly across personnel.

C. Being insensitive to the fact that in addition to the evaluation process being fair and equitable, it must be perceived as such by all concerned.

D. Failing to understand adequately the legal and ethical requirements governing personnel evaluation systems.

E. Ignoring or abusing the applicable substantive or procedural rights of participants during the evaluation process.

F. Failing to obtain timely, legal counsel in matters relating to participants' rights.

G. Failing to ensure that everyone concerned understands the operation of the personnel evaluation system, their rights, and their obligations.

Illustrative Case—Description A university required that each department provide annual evaluations of the faculty. The completed evaluations were prepared in letter form, submitted to the dean of the school, and used as part of the process for determining salary and promotion. The administration took the position that the individual department heads should be allowed maximum flexibility in determining their own procedures and criteria because different departments had different standards and needs. Consequently, faculty were confused and uneasy about the specific criteria by which they had been evaluated. Some department heads prepared evaluations without obtaining current information on faculty professional and scholarly activities. The results were a general sense of inequitable treatment, lowered morale, and a number of grievances.

Illustrative Case—Analysis The absence of clear formal guidelines at the university level resulted inevitably in variations in the criteria used and the procedures followed from department to department. Even within the same department, the lack of procedural guidelines allowed inconsistencies to occur from evaluation to evaluation. Under those conditions, an undermining sense of unfairness and inequity was bound to develop, and the entire evaluation process was harmed.

Illustrative Case—Suggestions Formal guidelines developed on a university level and within individual departments should have been provided and could have allowed for some clear variations based on differences in departmental standards and needs. Information on the criteria to be used should have been specified and made known to the faculty. Other procedures, including mandatory review of the evaluation with all evaluatees, also could have been included in the guidelines.

Supporting Documentation

American Association of School Personnel Administrators (1978).
Andrews, H. A. (1985).
French-Lazovik, G. (Ed.). (1982).
Landy, F. J., & Farr, J. L. (1983).
National Association of Elementary School Principals. (1984).
O'Dell, C. (1985).
Seldin, P. (1984).
Strike, K., & Bull, B. (1981).
Webb, L. D. (1983).

P-3 Conflict of Interest

> **STANDARD** Conflicts of interest should be identified and dealt with openly and honestly, so that they do not compromise the evaluation process and results.

Explanation Conflict of interest arises when an evaluator's own goals and biases exert, or might exert, inappropriate influence on a judgment or decision. It can intrude at several points in the personnel evaluation process: in designing the evaluation, selecting members for an evaluation committee, obtaining ratings of performance from students and supervisors, writing the evaluation report, and making decisions based on results. Frequently, conflicts of interest occur when an immediate supervisor's personal interests might be affected by the evaluation. Cases in which the supervisor is the sole evaluator are particularly subject to this problem.

Sources of conflict of interest are many and varied. By evaluating a person positively or negatively, the evaluator might obtain an advantage or disadvantage of position, realize better or poorer professional or personal relationships, or become vulnerable to retaliation. Moreover, the evaluation results might reflect upon the performance of the evaluator as well as the evaluatee. Other conflicts arise from differing philosophies of education, political preferences, and moral codes. Also, the reputation, status, or political influence of the evaluatee might be of concern to the evaluator. As a last example, the evaluator might be pressured or intimidated by leaders in the organization.

All evaluations are subject to such conflicts, and they must be controlled if the evaluation is to be fair and acceptable.

Rationale Conflict of interest can undermine the entire personnel evaluation system. The fidelity of the judgment is challenged when it is believed to have influenced the evaluation process and its result. Personnel decisions are placed in disrepute if the belief exists that any evaluation results are influenced or determined by personal self-interest, rather than organizational or professionally shared goals.

Guidelines

A. Encourage the cooperative development of evaluation designs that reduce the possibility of conflict of interest.

B. Specify common sources of conflict of interest in written evaluation program guidelines, and provide appeal procedures wherein alleged conflict of interest can be investigated and addressed. (See P-2.)

C. Make every effort to rule out conflict of interest and the appearance of it in order to ensure confidence in fairness, objectivity, and equity in the process and the outcome.

D. Exercise control of conflict of interest at every level of examination and judgment, including:

— Selection of personnel to conduct the process
— Use of clear criteria and objective evidence
— Involvement of the evaluatee and the client in the review process prior to finalizing the report
— Review of findings upon appeal
— Defining the range of evidence admitted into the review

E. Employ evaluation procedures requiring comparison of multiple sources of information to discover any tainted evidence.

F. Discuss in the evaluation report how the data used in judging the performance of individuals is related to the evaluation's purposes and criteria. (See U-4.)

G. Give first priority to using another evaluator if an unresolvable conflict of interest exists.

H. Mutually define, in writing, the conditions of the evaluation to include role-specific behavior assessed under defined conditions if an unresolvable conflict of interest exists, and it is impossible to appoint another evaluator.

I. Invite the evaluatee to append a reaction to the evaluation report. (See U-4.)

Common Errors

A. Failing to anticipate and control subjectivity; for example, by evaluating without specifically defined criteria.

B. Failing to define the conditions under which the evaluation will be considered valid.

C. Making assessment and evaluation the sole responsibility of one individual, without the possibility of appeal.

Illustrative Case #1—Description   A teacher received a poor evaluation from his school principal. Since in previous years he had received very positive evaluations, he was puzzled by the negative review and confused by the ambiguity of its contents. He tried unsuccessfully to obtain a clear, satisfactory explanation from his evaluator, and insisted that the evaluation be reviewed by a third party. The teacher and the principal were generally considered two of the district's outstanding employees. The teacher was unaware that they were competing for an administrative position at another, more desirable school, and a negative review at this time would adversely affect his opportunity for promotion.

Illustrative Case #1—Analysis   The teacher was unaware of the conflict of interest existing between him and his evaluator, and that it affected his assessment. A subsequent investigation revealed the promotional situation, which the principal denied had biased his review. However, he was still unable to substantiate his negative judgments stated on the evaluation. The competition seemed to have made the evaluator far more critical, seriously affecting the teacher's morale, potential performance, and career opportunities. The evaluator and the evaluation process were compromised.

Illustrative Case #1—Suggestions   The evaluator should have removed himself from that role in order to avoid the compromising situation or should have been removed by a superior. He should have demonstrated greater regard for fair process and for the rights of the evaluatee, and he should have recognized that the circumstances would, at best, create the appearance of a conflict of interest. The system should have assured judgments of the teacher's performance based on accepted educational practice and defensible criteria. It should have included safeguards for the integrity of evaluations, and an appeal process guaranteeing the right to an impartial investigation of conflict of interest charges.

Illustrative Case #2—Description   A classroom teacher was promoted to the assistant principalship of the elementary school where he had taught for six years. During those years, he had become good friends with another member of the staff whom he would now have the responsibility of evaluating. The new assistant principal asked one of the central office personnel to serve in his stead on the evaluation team with the principal. The resulting evaluation was completed, the assistant principal informed of the results, and the teacher directed toward the assistant principal for help in improving several areas of weakness.

Illustrative Case #2—Analysis The evaluation process described in this case avoided the conflict of interest issue by removing the potential source and by involving other evaluative personnel. However, one aspect of the procedure could not be handled otherwise: the involvement of the new assistant principal in fostering the improvements that were recommended by the evaluators. The new assistant principal could still work as an instructional leader, but the burden of judgment had been shifted to an objective colleague.

Illustrative Case #2—Suggestions Supervisors can assist subordinates to examine and address their performance deficiencies, even when the subordinates are friends or relatives. But to provide such assistance effectively, the supervisor must squarely address the potential conflicts of interest. To ameliorate these possible conflicts, the supervisor could take such steps as the following:

1. Replace himself in assessing and judging an employee's performance with a disinterested but otherwise qualified evaluator, which he did.

2. Meet with the evaluatee and the replacement evaluator prior to the evaluation to clarify and examine the evaluation questions and procedures, who would be performing the different evaluation tasks, and their qualifications.

3. Provide guidance for staff development based on the written evaluation report.

Supporting Documentation

Blumberg, A. (1980).
Landy, F. J., Barnes-Farell, J., & Cleveland, J. N. (1980).
Landy, F. J., Barnes, J. L., & Murphy, K. R. (1978).
Millman, J. (Ed.). (1981).
Soar, R. S., Medley, D. M., & Coker, H. (1983).

P-4 Access to Personnel Evaluation Reports

> **STANDARD** Access to reports of personnel evaluation should be limited to individuals with a legitimate need to review and use the reports, so that appropriate use of the information is assured.

Explanation Much of the information in personnel evaluation reports is of such a nature that access to it must be restricted to those persons with a professional need to see and use the reports. Such persons include the evaluatees themselves and those in positions officially authorized to make decisions and take actions based on the reports. Those auditing an evaluation also should have access to pertinent data and reports with individual identifications removed.

Appropriate use should be clearly defined in master agreements, individual contracts, and school board policies. (See P-2.) It would include guidance for staff development, remediation, or recognition; guidance for personnel actions as specified in formal agreements and policies; and record-keeping and accountability. (See U-2.) Appropriate use should be defined to apply only to the professional role(s) for which the evaluatee is employed or might be employed in the future. (See A-1.)

Rationale Access to personnel evaluation reports is a highly sensitive issue. The information in these reports typically is an important factor in such major decisions as whether or not one will be rewarded or promoted, keep a particular job, or continue to practice a given profession. Even when the use is for staff development or recognition, judgments of one's professional performance, when exposed to unauthorized parties, can be embarrassing or damaging.

Conversely, relevant information must not be withheld from those responsible for making important personnel judgments and decisions. Without it, inaccurate and unjust decisions may be made that serve poorly the evaluatee, the organization, students, and the community.

Guidelines

A. Reference the data and other information used as the basis of an evaluation in the written evaluation report or its appendix. (See U-4.)

B. Write CONFIDENTIAL at the top of an evaluation report and make no more copies than necessary.

C. Sign and date the original copy of the evaluation report.

D. Provide the evaluatee with a copy of the signed evaluation report including any appendixes.

E. If multiple copies of evaluation reports are maintained, ensure that they are identical.

F. Establish an official personnel file for each employee.

G. Discuss derogatory material with an employee before placing it in the official personnel file.

H. Notify an evaluatee in writing when the institution has added to her or his file sensitive or possibly controversial information or documents, except as otherwise provided for by laws or agreements.

I. Provide each evaluatee continuing opportunity to review the employee's personnel file; to append, within appropriate time restraints, written comments; and to request a copy of any item contained in the file, except as otherwise provided for by laws or agreements.

J. Specify in writing that, subject to statutory limitations, access, retrieval, and release of evaluation reports should be limited to persons with a legitimate need to know; e.g.:

— The evaluatee
— The evaluator
— The immediate supervisor
— Those who must make or defend decisions based on the results
— Prospective employers, higher education admissions officials, awards committees, or other such groups authorized by the evaluatee to receive the information
— Support personnel officially assigned and trained to produce, control, and retrieve personnel records

K. Make arrangements for secure storage of evaluation reports and other evaluation records. (See A-6.)

L. Specify, for any electronic storage of personnel records, procedures, rights, and safeguards which parallel the manual procedures for accessing and handling written personnel records.

M. Provide written instructions and inservice training to persons charged with implementing the evaluation system regarding access, retrieval, and release of evaluation records, and regarding the circumstances under which reports may be destroyed.

N. Certify in writing the support staff assigned to help produce, control, and retrieve personnel records; provide them with clear instructions regarding confidentiality and the control of records; restrict unauthorized personnel from seeing or reproducing the records.

O. Maintain records of report access, retrieval, or release, including the names of persons receiving records and the purposes for each release, and maintain a list of personnel authorized to have access to the file.

Common Errors

A. Failing to distinguish between a legitimate need to have access to an evaluation report and an expressed need based on curiosity or some other inappropriate purpose.

B. Granting access to persons of some standing but with no legitimate need to see a file or a report.

C. Failing to give timely notice when new information is added to an employee's file.

Illustrative Case—Description   A school district implemented a new career ladder plan. Among the criteria for achieving master teacher status was one requiring no less than "excellent" evaluation ratings in each of the three successive years preceding application. The competition became intense.

When one evaluatee was informed that her application would not be considered because she had received one "satisfactory" evaluation two years previously, she asked to review her evaluation report, knowing that the ratings had been excellent in all three years. She discovered that her records had been altered. When she asked the records clerk who had received the records, she was told they had been released to a teacher in her building who said she was serving on a personnel committee. The clerk did not know the person's name.

Illustrative Case—Analysis Apparently district policy on authorizing use of evaluation reports was either unclear, unenforced, or nonexistent. Personnel maintaining the records seemed not to have been instructed on conditions under which reports should be released, and there was no written record on who received reports and for what purposes. Under those conditions, it was difficult, if not impossible, to reconstruct what had occurred; and this experience created anxiety and lack of confidence among the rest of the school staff.

Illustrative Case—Suggestions The district should have developed a clear, specific, written policy on security and release of evaluation reports. All personnel responsible for the safekeeping and release of reports should have received training for their roles and been provided with written instructions on storage and release of reports. A system should have been established by which records were maintained of those who received access to evaluation files and for what purposes, including requiring that identification be presented, records be signed out and in, and up-to-date lists of authorized persons be maintained.

Supporting Documentation

Andrews, H. A. (1985).
Block, J. R. (1981).
Christina School District. (1984).
Christina School District. (1986).
O'Dell, C. (1985).

P-5 Interactions with Evaluatees

> **STANDARD**   The evaluation should address evaluatees in a professional, considerate, and courteous manner so that their self-esteem, motivation, professional reputations, performance, and attitude toward personnel evaluation are enhanced or, at least, not needlessly damaged.

Explanation   The evaluator must be cognizant of and responsive to the evaluatee's personal and professional needs. It is important to develop rapport, be professional, and follow institutional protocol. The evaluator must demonstrate a genuine interest in the evaluatee as a person who can gain competence from valid evaluative feedback and who, in turn, can provide improved professional service.

Rationale   The benefits of meeting this standard are pervasive throughout the evaluation process. When the evaluator and evaluatee share a sense of professionalism and basic human dignity, they are less likely to be anxious and feel negative toward the evaluation. When the approach is sensitive and professional, findings are more likely to be presented and received as constructive and oriented to professional growth. When evaluation is conducted in that manner, both the morale of the employee and the credibility of the evaluation process are likely to be enhanced. When negative findings are presented clearly, objectively, and privately, the employee is more likely to judge the process as fair and the evaluator as considerate. Overall, the exercise of good human relations can support the evaluatee's sense of worth and professionalism, foster better service, and strengthen the credibility of personnel evaluation.

Guidelines

A. Provide adequate time before formal assessment for early interaction among all participants in an evaluation, to develop mutual trust and understanding. (See F-2.)

B. Require evaluators and evaluatees to seek mutually acceptable goals and time lines, and encourage them to establish a productive, cooperative relationship.

C. Provide periodic training to evaluators in human relations procedures.

D. Monitor the effectiveness of the evaluation system regularly through systematic collection of process feedback from evaluatees. (See A-8.)

E. Schedule evaluation activities well in advance and stick to the schedule.

F. Conduct evaluation feedback sessions in private settings.

G. Use encouragement as a leadership tool.

Common Errors

A. Failing to create the conditions for timely and constructive interaction between evaluatees and evaluators.

B. Allowing evaluation feedback sessions to be interrupted by telephone calls or walk-in visitors.

C. Showing a general lack of respect for an employee whose work has been poor.

D. Engaging in public disparagement of employees.

Illustrative Case #1—Description   The Director of Admissions at a small liberal arts college was about to be evaluated. The evaluator was an administrator who had responsibility for all student records and services. Because of their busy schedules, neither person saw much of the other except for the occasional staff meetings, even though admissions was an area that the college needed to improve. The administrator perceived admissions as a necessary but non-academic salesmanship function, and did not hide that perception.

When the admissions director arrived for his evaluation, the administrator waved him into the office but continued to work at the papers on her desk. Without referring to any formal, written evaluation, the administrator stated that she "supposed" the Director had done "as good a job as could be expected, considering the nature of the student pool" and that "at least the Admissions Office had managed to maintain the entering class's size at nearly the same level as the prior year." She stated that the Director had at least found some warm bodies to fill the slots.

Illustrative Case #1—Analysis   The evaluator appeared to consider the admissions recruitment program as a distasteful aspect of her office responsibilities. Her attitude toward the admissions director lacked professionalism and collegiality and strongly conveyed her lack of respect for both the director and his work. The evaluation reflected no understanding of the difficulty and importance of the evaluatee's job, and no recognition or support of his efforts. It was bound to engender negative consequences.

Illustrative Case #1—Suggestions   To begin with, the college—knowing how the particular administrator felt about the admissions function—should never have appointed her to do the evaluation. The administrator, knowing her own attitude, could have declined to be the evaluator. Once she had agreed to undertake that role, however, she should have accepted the marketing-oriented admissions program as a bona fide method of recruitment and approached the task of evaluating the director's performance on that basis, according him the respect and consideration she·would have given a teaching member of the faculty. The college administration should have stressed the need for professional courtesy when it provided human relations orientation training for all evaluators in the college.

Illustrative Case #2—Description   A research and development center in a large university had received a grant that required the creation of a new position. A testing expert from a community college was selected over several internal applicants.

The university administration subsequently required that job descriptions for all positions in the center be updated, including the new position, even though the job description had recently been updated when the new incumbent had been hired. However, not all of the duties of the post had been determined at that time, so the bureaucratic requirement for redefinition did afford an opportunity for clarification and was at least a mixed blessing. The professor and his supervisor were given two weeks to update the job description. Both recognized the importance of the task and set out to do the best possible job. At the end of the two-week period, a description was approved that satisfied the professor, his supervisor, and the university administrators. The supervisor was to conduct a quarterly evaluation of the performance of the testing expert.

The new staff member enjoyed the challenge of his work in the center and excelled at his duties. Consequently, he was awarded high ratings by the supervisor in the first quarterly evaluation.

Hearing of the high ratings through contact with the dean, another testing expert in the college became annoyed and professionally jealous. She had applied unsuccessfully for the research post, and now saw the new "high flyer" as a threat to her status in the institution. The disgruntled professor channeled her concerns into her role as a member of the university's Personnel Evaluation Committee. At an opportune time in one of the committee meetings, she convinced her colleagues on the committee to call for a special audit of the project position.

After five months on the job, the supervisor and testing expert were informed, with a vague explanation, that the personnel department would conduct a special audit of the job. Both were required to fill out voluminous questionnaires, but neither one was interviewed. A member of the personnel department, who had never met the supervisor or the incumbent, rewrote the job description, and the department downgraded the salary rating of the job. A letter giving only the new numerical rating was sent to the testing expert.

He became angry and felt that he could not trust his co-workers. His morale suffered. Both he and his supervisor demanded an appeal, and, after a lengthy process, involving observations and interviews, the original rating was restored. However, the relationship between the center and the personnel department was strained; and the testing expert lost some of his enthusiasm for working at the university.

Illustrative Case #2—Analysis By allowing gossip by disgruntled employees to sway their actions, the administration violated the rules of conduct expected of professionals. In addition, it is doubtful that the special and demoralizing audit was justified, since no explanation for it was given to the testing expert or his supervisor. Finally, as part of a fair, professional assessment, he should have been interviewed and observed at work. In general, the administration erred badly by not communicating clearly and professionally with the evaluatee and the supervisor, and, in doing so, needlessly created disruption and discontent.

Illustrative Case #2—Suggestions The procedures for evaluating the performance of the testing expert and/or for changing his job description should have been established by the administration at the outset. Strict guidelines should have been adhered to, and the administrators should not have been swayed by gossip. Something as disruptive as a special audit should have been pursued only if the case for doing so was clear and persuasive. Lines of communication between the involved parties should have been kept open. The testing expert should have been informed of the reason for the audit, and, if one was needed, he and his supervisor should have been consulted by the person rewriting the job description. Somewhere in the process, the administration might have congratulated the new employee for having earned high ratings.

Supporting Documentation

Acheson, K., & Gall, M. (1980).
Blumberg, A. (1980).
Educational Research Services. (1974).
Evertson, C. M., & Holley, F. M. (1981).
McGreal, T. (1983).
Medley, D. M., Coker, H., & Soar, R. S. (1984).
Millman, J. (Ed.). (1981).
Strike, K., & Bull, B. (1981).
Wise, A. E., & Darling-Hammond, L. (1985).

Utility Standards

Summary of the Standards

U Utility Standards The Utility Standards are intended to guide evaluations so that they will be informative, timely, and influential.

U1 Constructive Orientation Evaluations should be constructive, so that they help institutions to develop human resources and encourage and assist those evaluated to provide excellent service.

U2 Defined Uses The users and the intended uses of a personnel evaluation should be identified, so that the evaluation can address appropriate questions.

U3 Evaluator Credibility The evaluation system should be managed and executed by persons with the necessary qualifications, skills, and authority, and evaluators should conduct themselves professionally, so that evaluation reports are respected and used.

U4 Functional Reporting Reports should be clear, timely, accurate, and germane, so that they are of practical value to the evaluatee and other appropriate audiences.

U5 Follow-Up and Impact Evaluations should be followed up, so that users and evaluatees are aided to understand the results and take appropriate actions.

U-1 *Constructive Orientation*

STANDARD Evaluations should be constructive, so that they help institutions to develop human resources and encourage and assist those evaluated to provide excellent service.

Explanation Evaluations are constructive when they promote the success of students, educators, and organizations. They are constructive when they guide selection and retention of competent personnel, reinforce good practice, provide direction for improving performance, clarify needs for professional development, recognize outstanding performance, assist in terminating incompetent personnel, promote professionalism, and foster collegiality and harmony.

Evaluations are not constructive if they are perfunctory responses to bureaucratic requirements for accountability, are used essentially to control or intimidate, or are used as political instruments.

Rationale When personnel evaluation is constructive, it encourages and supports educators and their organization to fulfill their goals and responsibilities. Educators are provided with information and reactions that enrich their professional self-knowledge, increase their enthusiasm, and enhance their efficacy as practitioners. Organizations are aided in selecting and retaining competent personnel, reinforcing strong professional practice, encouraging professional development, and fostering cooperation. Educators and institutions that achieve such beneficial characteristics are thereby enabled to provide superior services to students and to maintain their effectiveness and positive self-image through periods of stability or change.

Evaluations that emphasize negative assessments and results discourage educators and engender resistance to evaluation and institutional goals. Evaluations that identify performance weaknesses but do not provide information or support to correct deficiencies contribute little to the individual or the organization.

Guidelines

A. Involve a representative group of evaluation participants in designing and developing the personnel evaluation system, including the definition of performance standards and the roles to be played by interested parties. (See P-2 and F-2.)

B. Secure the governing board's support for the personnel evaluation system.

C. Communicate to all interested parties the intended positive, constructive uses of evaluation results; conceptualize personnel evaluation as an important part of professional development and achievement of organizational goals.

D. Create a shared understanding among interested parties of the purpose and procedures of the personnel evaluation system. (See U-2 and F-2.)

E. Define and clarify performance standards for all professional positions. (See A-1.)

F. Provide timely evaluation feedback. (See U-4.)

G. Begin evaluation conferences on a positive note, avoiding an adversarial posture and emphasizing support for the evaluatee as a professional and promotion of professional growth and improvement.

H. Identify performance areas for reinforcement and improvement.

I. Provide specific constructive ways to overcome deficiencies.

J. Use evaluations to allocate resources for improving performance, and provide resources and support for that purpose.

K. Encourage, train, and assist educators to assess and improve their own performance.

Common Errors

A. Assuming that personnel evaluation practices, procedures, and objectives are self-explanatory and acceptable.

B. Failing to recognize and respond to both strengths and weaknesses of an evaluatee's professional qualifications or performance.

C. Failing to assess whether the educator is provided with sufficient resources and support to do the job.

D. Fostering competition among individuals to the detriment of collegiality and teamwork.

E. Making unreasonable recommendations for improvement.

Illustrative Case #1—Description   A school district divided a merit pay fund among its schools in proportion to the number of teachers in each school. All teachers were informed in September that 25 percent of the teachers in each school would be given merit pay. The merit stipend would be based on the performance of their students on achievement goals to be negotiated with the school principal. As a result, teachers became secretive and competitive, and some tried to establish performance standards that would be easy to meet. During the year, teaching in some classes was concentrated on the content of the achievement tests to be used and on those students considered least likely to meet the performance standards. The merit pay evaluation stimulated negative reactions from some parents, who thought their normally high-achieving children were being shortchanged, and from some teachers, who thought the new level of competitiveness among teachers was divisive and lowering school morale.

Illustrative Case #1—Analysis   This case illustrates some of the hazards of evaluations that compare professionals. Such evaluations can divide rather than unify colleagues and appeal to selfish interests rather than promote enhanced professional performance. If applied constructively and sensitively, this opportunity to make merit pay awards had the potential for clarifying performance goals, motivating teachers to demonstrate appropriate goal achievement, and recognizing and reinforcing good service. But, misapplied, as in this case, the evaluation induced divisiveness, lowering of standards, and disservice to students.

Illustrative Case #1—Suggestions   In order to achieve the potential benefits of the merit pay evaluation without incurring the negative side effects noted above, this district could have invoked a procedure likely to enhance performance and greater collegiality. They could have focused the merit pay pool not on individual teachers but on schools or teams of teachers, thereby encouraging cooperation within the schools or teams. They also could have precluded some of the unforeseen negative consequences by involving teachers in the design of the plan and soliciting their suggestions and judgments before and during its implementation.

Illustrative Case #2—Description   Enthusiastic about the idea of merit pay, the Board of Trustees and the President of a state university decided to conduct a special evaluation of faculty. Accordingly, the President asked department chairpersons to nominate at least one but not more than five percent of their faculty for a merit pay award. Chairpersons were asked to submit their nominations within two weeks of the request and to maintain silence about their nominations to avoid any delay or disruption of the process.

When the nominations were submitted, the President and deans selected faculty and made their choices public, first to the faculty in a special news release and then to the community through the local newspaper.

The reaction of faculty was one of general outrage toward the evaluation process, their exclusion, and the response to their subsequent complaints in a heated environment. When faculty asked, for example, "What does one do to deserve merit?" the reply was, "You know who the merit faculty are and why they are the best. Read their publications and go sit in one of their classrooms and see what they do." Those who didn't receive merit awards believed they were worthy, resented the secrecy, and felt that their contributions to the university were not recognized or appreciated.

Illustrative Case #2—Analysis The Board, the deans, and the President failed to involve the department chairpersons and faculty in planning the award program. The advice and support of department chairpersons and faculty were neither sought nor considered. Chairpersons were informed of the purpose of the evaluation, but given no guidance as to the criteria, standards, and procedures to be used. Faculty were excluded, except as the objects of evaluation, and not even informed that the process was occurring.

The deans and the President demonstrated little awareness of faculty sensitivities or professional role. The evaluation permitted criteria and standards to vary from department to department, which encouraged a sense of unfairness. And their secrecy was bound to engender fear and distrust. The evaluation process, in short, stood as little more than an apparent pretext for permitting the deans and President to make awards, and it transformed an opportunity into a costly, demoralizing experience.

Illustrative Case #2—Suggestions Full employee involvement is as important as a strong executive desire for efficient and effective personnel evaluation programs. Cooperation among university executives, college and department administrators, and faculty in planning an evaluation program is essential to promote respect and acceptance for its outcomes.

The President or his administrative representatives could have worked openly with faculty to explore the need and direction for change in the faculty evaluation system and the purposes it might serve. The President could have requested faculty participation in the planning of the program and sought their agreement on the purpose, instruments, and procedures. If the value of the program to the organization was suspect, it could have been reconsidered and revised before implementation.

Involvement of employees would have increased the information faculty had and given them the opportunity to shape a program so as to be amenable to both their professional values and their need for recognition.

Supporting Documentation

Brock, S. C. (1981).

Educational Research Service, Inc. (1985).

French-Lazovik, G. (Ed.). (1982).

Iwanicki, E. F. (1981).

Landy, F. J., Barnes, J. L. & Murphy, K. R. (1978).

Landy, F. J., Barnes-Farell, J., & Cleveland, J. N. (1980).

McGreal, T. (1983).

Morrison, J., & O'Hearne, J. (1977).

Oliver, B. (1982).

Redfern, G. B. (1980).

Robertson, M. J. (1973).

Wise, A. E., Darling-Hammond, L., McLaughlin, M., & Bernstein, H. T. (1984).

STANDARD The users and the intended uses of a personnel evaluation should be identified, so that the evaluation can address appropriate questions.

Explanation Evaluation planners should identify and consult with each user group to clarify the purposes of the evaluation. The prospective users may include administrators, board members, faculty, accrediting agents, students, and others with legitimate interests in evaluation results. Typical uses are to meet the demands of selection, certification, diagnosis of staff development needs, accountability, promotion, awarding tenure, salary determination, recognition, and terminating employment.

Rationale Personnel evaluations should be guided by their intended use. This requires that the users be identified and consulted, their information needs be specified, and information uses be clarified. Only then can the evaluator correctly determine the evaluation questions, the behavior to be observed and assessed, the products to be examined, and the reports to be issued. Identification of intended uses also safeguards against information misuse. Information created for one purpose may be inappropriate when applied to another, as each purpose may involve unique questions and require particular information.

Information applied for other than intended use also may produce damaging side effects. If this standard is not met, individuals may come to distrust the evaluation system. They may also withhold information, believing that it may be misused or will serve no legitimate purpose.

Guidelines

A. Identify and consult potential audiences, especially primary users, to clarify their needs for personnel evaluation information.

B. Invite the evaluatees to help determine evaluation goals, uses, forms, methods, and audiences. (See F-2.)

C. Construct evaluation questions that are relevant to information needs and proposed uses.

D. Reach formal agreements with all parties involved to assure that they understand and are committed to the intended use of the evaluation information. (See P-2.)

E. Formally determine which users are authorized to see what information and enforce the restrictions. (See P-2 and P-4.)

F. Monitor the evaluation process to ensure tight connections between the collected information, intended uses, and actual uses. (See A-8.)

Common Errors

A. Assuming that all users have identical or similar needs that will be met by the same type of information.

B. Assuming too narrow or broad an audience and uses for the evaluations.

C. Making unilateral decisions about which data will be most useful for which users.

D. Determining how information will be used after, rather than before, it has been collected and reviewed.

E. Ignoring restrictions on the use of given information or not adequately policing its use.

F. Not documenting agreements on intended use. (See P-2.)

Illustrative Case #1—Description   The principal of an elementary school, a firm believer in using evaluation to improve performance, sought the assistance of the district evaluator in designing a system that could be used for coaching teachers. The stated purpose of the evaluation was to help each teacher identify performance strengths and weaknesses in leading class discussions and to set goals for improvement. The evaluator and the principal assured the teachers that the evaluation's sole purpose was to help each teacher and that the teachers would be the sole users. Teachers were also assured that they would not be compared with other teachers, but would have private use of the information about themselves to improve their performance and set goals. The principal would contribute to the evaluation information but would not control it.

The evaluator constructed a checklist of teacher behaviors, that the teachers accepted with modifications. The checklist was to be filled out on each teacher by the principal and one other teacher.

The faculty was divided into pairs of teachers. The principal observed each teacher, then took over their classes, allowing the members of each pair to observe each other, meet to review assessment data, and then coach one another.

The initial observations were made, goals were set, and coaching for improvement occurred from January through April. The evaluator could see good results as measured by changes in classroom discussions and by structured interviews with the teachers and principal.

In May, the principal was required to rank the teachers in the building for pink-slipping necessitated by reduced funding and enrollment declines. Whereas most principals in the system rank ordered on the basis of seniority, this principal, armed with the teacher evaluation information, used it for this unintended purpose. The principal assured the teachers that the competence ranking was based only partly on the performance improvement data. The teachers nevertheless refused to participate further in the project.

Illustrative Case #1—Analysis   This case illustrates the problems of using personnel evaluation information to serve unintended uses. The evaluator and principal, at the outset, should have ensured that the information would not be used in ways other than those promised. When an outside circumstance—the probable need for layoffs—required the rank ordering of teachers, the principal was faced with a difficult choice. She could have followed the safe course and ranked teachers according to seniority—an objective procedure. However, the principal believed that some of the least senior teachers were more effective than some of the more senior teachers, and that the evaluation data she needed to support her view were available only through the improvement evaluation program. She concluded that while the evaluation data did not directly address her needs, it was now relevant and helpful to use the information that the teachers had compiled on themselves.

Illustrative Case #1—Suggestions   Proper safeguards should have been established to assure that the evaluation information would be used only for the purposes intended. The principal should not have used the evaluation information to rank order the teachers. Under the conditions of the adopted evaluation plan, the parties to the evaluation could have signed a memorandum of agreement (see P-2) confirming the rules for using the evaluation data. Such a formal agreement would have precluded violation of the rules, retained the faculty's confidence in the principal, and extended a successful collaborative effort to improve faculty effectiveness in the classroom.

Illustrative Case #2—Description In a university student counseling department, a performance evaluation program was developed and implemented with the understanding among evaluatees, supervisors, and administrators that the results would be used to set goals for the evaluatees. The evaluations would report specific performance problems and suggest methods for correction. The evaluations were to be conducted semiannually and no numeric values were to be attached to the results. The program was dropped after two years, but resulted in four evaluations for most of the employees. When the program was terminated, most of the related files were discarded, including the stated purposes and conditions. However, the evaluation results for employees were retained. Approximately one year after the program was discontinued, a new administrator discovered copies of the evaluation reports and found them instructive for ranking candidates for promotion. The administrator, needing information by which to assess candidates, attached scores to the evaluations and used the scores to reach promotion decisions.

Illustrative Case #2—Analysis This example demonstrates how serious problems can result from the failure to be clear about the intended use of evaluations and to honor this intention. The information needed to make sound promotion decisions clearly might differ from that which would be germane to staff development. In the latter case, evaluators might appropriately concentrate on performance problems; but, though they should also reinforce an evaluatee's strengths, these could be ignored or minimized. This deficiency would become a serious flaw if the purpose of the evaluation changed from staff development to some other end, such as promotion. The most likely consequences of such a change of purpose are diminished trust in the evaluation system and unwarranted decisions either for or against promotion. While the new administrator might have been unaware of the circumstances surrounding the collection of the performance data, the organization was still responsible for honoring its promises to members. In this case, its actions communicated a message to its employees that promises might not be kept and that evaluations emphasized negative data.

Illustrative Case #2—Suggestions   Documenting the entire appraisal process, including its approved uses and conditions, is essential. When an organization collects data about its employees, it must record and retain the policies that govern the use of the data. If the new administrator had known of the specific purposes and procedures of the performance appraisals, as well as its results, he and the evaluated employees might have been protected from damaging misuse of the information.

Supporting Documentation

Carroll, S. J., & Schneier, C. E. (1982).
Lacho, K. J., Stearns, G. K., & Billere, M. F. (1979).
Lee, R. D., Jr. (1979).
Locher, A., & Teel, R. (1977).
McGreal, T. L. (1982).
Peterson, K. (1984).
Smith, H., & Brouwer, P. (1977).

U-3 Evaluator Credibility

> **STANDARD** The evaluation system should be managed and executed by persons with the necessary qualifications, skills, sensitivity, and authority, and evaluators should conduct themselves professionally, so that evaluation reports are respected and used.

Explanation Institutions should take great care in appointing, training, supporting, and monitoring the persons who manage and implement personnel evaluation systems. Only appropriately qualified evaluators should be placed in charge, and their authority and responsibility to conduct valid and reliable personnel evaluations should be clearly established. Administrators, faculty, and others who implement evaluation plans should be trained in the institution's specific evaluation policies and procedures.

Assessment of an evaluatee's content or discipline qualifications must be made by someone with the pertinent expertise. For example, when administrators evaluate teachers' knowledge of subject matter fields, often they should supplement their judgments with those of content experts. When students are asked to assess instructors, or employees to assess supervisors, they should be given a standard procedure and clear instructions.

Those in charge of personnel evaluation should exercise utmost professionalism and sensitivity in planning, implementing, and reporting evaluations. Evaluators should be accountable for producing valid and reliable data and for justifying their conclusions and recommendations. Evaluation feedback sessions should be systematic and follow a specific agenda. The institution should monitor the evaluation system (see A-8) and hold evaluators accountable for competent fulfillment of their evaluation responsibilities.

Rationale The acceptance of an evaluation depends heavily upon the evaluatee's perceptions of the evaluator's authority, expertise, professionalism, sensitivity, trustworthiness, and efficient and effective performance. If evaluators are not viewed as credible—having the authority to evaluate, being knowledgeable about the evaluatee's position and field of expertise, and free of conflict of interest--evaluatees may be uncooperative and resist or attack the use of evaluation reports related to their employment. Credible evaluators, on the other hand, strengthen the process and contribute to its constructive use.

Guidelines

A. Assign evaluation roles to educators with appropriate professional training and skills, professionalism and sensitivity, and who understand the evaluation tasks and the roles of the personnel to be evaluated.

B. Ensure that evaluators of classroom practice understand effective teaching techniques and principles of learning psychology.

C. Train administrators, board members, faculty, and evaluation specialists to be effective in their role in the institution's evaluation system.

D. Train those who will serve as evaluators in principles of sound personnel evaluation, performance appraisal techniques, methods for motivating faculties, conflict management, and the law as it applies to education personnel evaluation.

E. Establish the authority and responsibilities of the evaluators.

F. When feasible, engage an evaluation team rather than a single administrator, to enhance credibility and validity.

G. Provide evaluators with support personnel or services to assist in collecting and analyzing needed information when those tasks exceed their professional training and expertise.

H. Require that evaluators be responsible for their evaluation assignments from start to finish; substitutes in midstream are vulnerable and not well received.

I. Prepare and use a relevant agenda for evaluation feedback sessions, if they are held. Such an agenda might include:

— Review the job description, prior objectives, accomplishments, and strengths and weaknesses
— Develop an action plan, including institutional support
— Schedule a follow-up evaluation
— Ask the evaluatee to summarize the feedback, discussion, targets for improvement, and next steps
— Promise and deliver a written summary

J. Exercise professionalism in reporting on and discussing the performance of a staff member, e.g.:

— Discuss the evaluation only in a professional setting
— Present facts
— Be open to gathering additional information if it is needed
— Avoid discussing personalities

K. Stress and demonstrate commitment to educational improvement. (See U-1.)

L. Promptly reinforce improvement by an educator involved in remediation.

M. Evaluate the work of each evaluator periodically. (See A-8.)

Common Errors

A. Defending and sustaining a weak or ineffective personnel evaluation system.

B. Failing to foster a climate of support and growth for evaluatees. (See P-5.)

C. Failing to plan and prepare carefully for observations and other evaluation activities.

D. Failing to implement scheduled evaluation activities as planned.

E. Producing imprecise or inaccurate written evaluation summaries.

F. Basing evaluation conclusions on preconceptions rather than valid information.

G. Failing to supply evaluatees with recommendations or services they can use to overcome identified deficiencies.

H. Discussing evaluation results with persons who have no professional reason to know them. (See P-4.)

Illustrative Case #1—Description The principal had scheduled performance evaluations starting with a new kindergarten teacher. He dreaded her performance evaluation because her class had been chaotic all year. He had spoken to her several times about her students wandering through the halls and the chaos that prevailed in her classroom. She had expressed little concern about knowledge objectives. "Kindergarten," she said, "should be mainly a socializing experience. Children should learn to get along with others, share, and cooperate, and that's enough to expect.'' The principal had planned to spend forty minutes filling out the teacher's performance evaluation form, but he got a number of phone calls and spent most of the morning cleaning up nagging details. So he completed the form in the last five minutes before going to lunch with the principal of the middle school. When that colleague arrived, he asked for some records, and the principal had to ransack his office to find them. Upon returning from lunch at 1:30 for his 1:00 appointment with the teacher, he found her waiting for him. The principal made small talk while he searched five minutes for her performance evaluation form. The teacher, of course, was irritated by the delay. Then, when he finally found the form, she was more disturbed by the evaluation. She was surprised and hurt that all the love she had lavished on her kindergarteners did not seem to count. The teacher said she got the impression that all the principal cared about was that the kids be kept quiet and at their seats all day. When he referred to the chaos, she retorted that it was hard to keep 26 five-year-olds quiet all day. The principal became flustered and said she would just have to do better next year. She became defensive and demanded that the principal explain what he would have done. The interview ended with the teacher in tears and the principal red in the face. As long as she stayed at Southern Primary School, she remembered and resented her evaluation experience.

Illustrative Case #1—Analysis This case illustrates the dangers of unplanned and careless performance evaluation interviews and how they can undermine the credibility of the evaluator. The principal did not base the evaluation on an official position description. He did not have the teacher do a self-assessment, so he could not identify any shared perceptions of performance. He was late for the interview, lost the performance evaluation form, and then gave a negative evaluation in global terms. His emotional criticism offered no guidance to the teacher on how to improve her performance. She became defensive and questioned the principal's motives and concern. What should have been a constructive exchange was a mutually harmful confrontation. The principal lost his credibility as an evaluator with this teacher, and colleagues she would talk to; and the teacher emerged with a jaundiced view of her principal and perhaps her profession.

Illustrative Case #1—Suggestions   In order to benefit from performance evaluation, the evaluatee must see the evaluator as a credible source of information. The performance evaluation interview must be conducted in an entirely professional manner. It must begin on time. The evaluator must prepare for the interview and offer specific examples of the evaluatee's strengths and weaknesses, which must be keyed to the position description. It is helpful for the evaluator to spend some time at the beginning of the interview going over the areas of agreement on performance to establish a shared perception of at least some of the performance. For those evaluatees who fall significantly below expectations, it is important to provide a formal, written performance improvement plan, complete with goals for improvement, dates by which the goals must be attained, institutional support to be provided, and evidence to be used in assessing progress.

Illustrative Case #2—Description   A community and technical college faced a need to select new faculty members. The college had experienced rapid growth and expansion, due to local industry's needs for workers trained in specific new technologies. The college had addressed the needs by adding 20 temporary, part-time faculty and assigning them to teach new courses and revise specific programs. These faculty member's assignments were keyed directly to the current needs of local industry. Based on performance evaluations, all but two of the part-time faculty members had effectively carried out their assignments.

While the college was addressing this current, local need, it also made a five-year projection of enrollments and concluded that the faculty should immediately be increased by 10%. Accordingly, the college launched a search for 30 new faculty members. A local businessman who served on the college board urged that new tenure-track positions be offered to 18 of the temporary, part-time faculty members, since their performance evaluations had been positive and since they were well liked and respected by local businessmen. The college president had misgivings about this recommendation but knew he would have to be careful in how he addressed it. His basic concern was that successful performance in a temporary assignment was not necessarily a guarantee of successful performance in a new tenure-track position that might have a different orientation. The former assignments were keyed to current, perhaps temporary needs, while the tenure-track positions had been defined in consideration of the college's mission and the five-year projection of needs. On the other hand, the part-time, temporary employees should be given due consideration. Also, the board member would expect an explanation if the college chose not to follow his recommendation.

The college president charged his personnel officer to design and implement a fair, valid, and politically viable procedure for selecting the new faculty members. The personnel officer did the following:

1. He formed an advisory committee with representatives from the board, the regular faculty, the administration, the part-time faculty, and local industry.

2. He established the principle that new faculty members would be selected based upon assessments of their qualifications to perform in explicitly defined tenure-track faculty positions.

3. He defined the overall assessment plan and obtained approval of the plan from the college administration and board of trustees.

4. He engaged the committee in reviewing and clarifying the job descriptions, defining the criteria for assessing the qualifications of applicants, determining which jobs could be clustered together, and nominating persons to assess applications for each cluster of jobs.

5. He selected and trained three-person teams to assess the applications for each cluster of jobs and then supervised their assessment activities.

6. He engaged an external evaluator to audit the personnel evaluation and selection process.

7. He reported the results of the assessments of applicants to the college president and provided him with the external evaluator's assessment of the process.

As a result of the process, the college president reported to the board on the personnel selection process, his nominations of 30 persons to be offered tenure-track positions, and on the external audit of the process. In response to a board member's question, the president said that all temporary faculty had been notified of the 30 positions, that ten of them had applied, that four of these persons were each ranked first in their group of applicants and were being recommended for tenure-track positions, and that the other six were not ranked first in their group. Several board members then commended the president and the personnel officer on the thorough, fair, effective, and accountable evaluation process. The board unanimously adopted the president's slate of nominees, and no temporary faculty member filed a grievance over not being offered a regular position.

Illustrative Case #2—Analysis   Both college officials and the part-time faculty members were satisfied with the evaluation. It was viewed as valid and fair for a number of important reasons:

— It was keyed to careful definitions of the jobs to be filled
— it was collaboratively planned
— Each application was rated by three assessors
— The assessors were trained to carry out their assignments
— The entire process was subjected to an external audit

Overall, the personnel officer established his credibility by carrying out the evaluation in a systematic and professional manner.

Illustrative Case #2—Suggestions   Administrators and evaluators should expect that board members and other influential persons will often make recommendations that reflect expedience or favoritism. They should also realize that evaluatees and other parties to the evaluation will more likely respect and accept potentially controversial findings and decisions if the evaluator has earned the respect and confidence of all affected parties. The best way to develop one's credibility as an evaluator is to carry out the evaluation in an entirely professional manner and then to offer conclusions and recommendations that are justified by the findings rather than political concerns. Involvement of the affected parties in planning the evaluation, keying it to explicit job descriptions, and subjecting it to the scrutiny of an external auditor are especially powerful steps to establishing one's credibility as a professional evaluator.

Supporting Documentation

Andrews, H. A. (1985).
Bellon, J. J. (1984).
Block, J. R. (1981).
Carroll, S. J., & Schneier, C. E. (1982).
Duke, D. L., & Stiggins, R. J. (1986).
Glasman, N. S. (n.d.).Grossnickle, D., & Cutter, T. (1984).
Heneman, H., Schwab, D., Fossum, J., & Dyer, L. (1983).

Medley, D. M., Coker, H., & Soar, R. S. (1984).

Millman, J. (Ed.). (1981).

Neagley, R., & Evans, N. D. (1980).

Smith, P. C. (1976).

Wise, A., Darling-Hammond, L., McLaughlin, M., & Bernstein, H. (1984).

U-4 Functional Reporting

STANDARD   Reports should be clear, timely, accurate, and germane, so that they are of practical value to the evaluatee and other appropriate audiences.

Explanation   To be useful, the information should be reported when the user needs it and when the evaluatee can best apply it to improve performance. The report should directly address the purposes of the evaluation and be keyed to the appropriate position description and standards. It should employ language and terms immediately understandable to all audiences, and should clearly delineate the practical implications of the evaluation data.

Feedback should be provided while recollections of behaviors are still fresh, affording opportunities for response and appeal and time to assist in improving performance.

The report should reflect agreed-upon job expectations and performance criteria (see A-1). A fair evaluation should reflect documented strengths and weaknesses of the assessed qualifications or performance to the extent that they exist.

Rationale   Since evaluation reports become the basis for important judgments about the practice, status, and development needs of professionals, they should provide clear, useful, and relevant information; and they should be provided at times and in ways that facilitate decision making and action.

Reports should not be ends in themselves, but instruments for achieving the purposes of the evaluation. They should assist and guide the evaluatee and other appropriate audiences to take relevant actions. Vague wording and recommendations diminish the worth of the evaluation.

Evaluations are often incorrectly slanted toward "faults" in an individual or toward giving unqualified praise. Both biases reduce the validity and utility of evaluation. Accuracy in reporting strengths and weaknesses helps to reduce systematic error in evaluations and is essential for stimulating and reinforcing improved performance.

Guidelines

A. Begin evaluations early to allow time for interim reporting.

B. Address only identified professional responsibilities in the evaluation report.

C. Write the report immediately following the observation, interview, or other data-gathering process, while the activity is still fresh in mind.

D. Write the report soon enough following an observation so that it can be provided to the evaluatee in advance of a post-observation conference.

E. Write the report to bear directly on the behavior or other indicators of status that reflect agreed-upon objectives and criteria.

F. Check the accuracy of data and the clarity and defensibility of the draft report. Consider involving the evaluatee or other appropriate users in the review process prior to finalizing the report.

G. Conduct feedback sessions to encourage evaluatee acceptance and use of the findings to improve performance.

H. Issue formal notices as intermediate and fair warnings that cited deficiencies must be remedied. (See P-1 and P-2.)

Common Errors

A. Not helping audiences to identify actions to be taken by or on behalf of the evaluatee.

B. Trying to please users of the evaluation by reflecting an individual's preconceived strengths or weaknesses.

C. Overemphasizing the importance of either strengths or weaknesses through the use of excessive, misleading detail.

D. Distorting the evaluation by seeking a numerical balance between positives and negatives.

E. Presenting a report as unanimous or reflecting consensus though the contributors failed to agree on findings and recommendations. (See A-4 and A-7.)

Illustrative Case—Description   A university student service office was having morale problems, and the agency head decided to identify and address the issues through employee evaluations. Since he preferred that the process not be too formal or official, he asked a faculty colleague and friend to serve as the evaluator; the colleague, a respected senior member of the faculty, had no experience as an evaluator beyond the usual service on tenure and promotion committees, but agreed, as a favor, to conduct the evaluation. She did not want to seem a representative of management, and so tried to be friendly and form informal relationships with the persons being evaluated. In addition, the evaluator was uneasy about officially recording employee problems and deficiencies. Consequently, her official report to the agency head was largely positive, and she communicated her negative impressions of the situation and certain employees in an informal session with the agency head. The employees were confused by the difference between the largely positive individual written reports they received and the negative treatment some were experiencing from the head, based on the information not included in those reports. Morale declined further, and the situation was exacerbated by the misuse of evaluations.

Illustrative Case—Analysis   The tendency of the evaluator to be positive in the written evaluations but to make negative informal reports destroyed the credibility of the evaluations, harmed the situation they were intended to relieve, and probably eliminated any future usefulness of evaluations in that office.

Illustrative Case—Suggestions   The evaluator should have made clear to the employees and agency head that the written evaluation reports would include both strengths and weaknesses and would constitute her complete report. And she should have conducted herself accordingly. The agency head erred in using an inexperienced and untrained evaluator, especially in a sensitive, negative situation. He should have determined whether the evaluator was capable of carrying out a frank, objective evaluation and producing a straightforward, accurate report. If the colleague did not meet those standards, he should have employed a qualified alternate.

Supporting Documentation

Andrews, H. A. (1985).
Duke, D. L., & Stiggins, R. J. (1986).
Greller, M. M., & Herold, D. M. (1975).
O'Dell, C. (1985).

U-5   Follow-Up and Impact

> **STANDARD**   Evaluations should be followed up, so that users and evaluatees are aided to understand the results and take appropriate actions.

Explanation   Those in charge of coordinating or conducting evaluations should not only reach sound assessments but should recognize that purpose and value lie in application of the findings. Consequently, they should help users understand the evaluations and pursue appropriate actions based on the evaluation results. For example, supervisors should work with evaluatees to design appropriate plans to assist evaluatees in overcoming assessed weaknesses and reinforcing strengths.

Rationale   Follow-up activities should be a natural outgrowth of the evaluation process. For example, merely describing to employees their performance in relation to a prescribed standard falls far short of the potential positive impact of a well-designed evaluation program on the evaluatee and the organization.

Guidelines

A. Review with the evaluatee the specific areas of strengths and weaknesses.

B. Give recognition to outstanding performance.

C. Include ways to improve identified weaknesses.

D. Solicit the evaluatee's suggestions for improving performance.

E. Develop, with the appropriate support personnel, a flexible professional growth plan to take advantage of assessed strengths or to overcome identified weaknesses.

F. Arrange follow-up conferences between the evaluatee and appropriate support personnel.

G. Assist the evaluatee with resources, released time, and/or other practical actions that may enable the professional growth plan to succeed.

H. Advise the evaluatee of the implications of success or failure in completing the professional growth plan.

I. Schedule the next evaluation.

J. Keep a record of instances in which the evaluatee did or did not act upon recommendations from evaluations.

K. Give any necessary notices of possible non-reemployment by the appropriate date.

L. Keep written records of the total process.

M. Use information in the manner prescribed in the adopted formal guidelines (see P-2) for making personnel decisions, such as selection and merit pay.

N. Work with users to be sure that they understand and make appropriate use of the evaluation information.

O. Determine necessary modifications in the evaluation procedure to increase evaluation use and impact on practice and outcomes. (See A-8.)

Common Errors

A. Prescribing activities in a professional growth plan that are unrealistic.

B. Failing to prioritize in the plan what is to be accomplished.

C. Allowing too much or too little time for completing all or any part of the plan.

D. Failing by the supervisor to keep superiors informed of serious performance problems when they are identified.

E. Failing to use the evaluation information appropriately in personnel decisions.

F. Assuming that all appropriate users will understand and will use the information.

Illustrative Case—Description   A high school language arts teacher had been in the district for 16 years. Information in his personnel file indicated that a conference concerning poor class discipline was held with him in the second semester of his second year and again in his third year, when he was granted tenure. In the next 13 years, three principals and the language arts department coordinator contributed an additional five conference summaries to his personnel file. The summaries cited poor class control, poor motivational techniques, inappropriate subject matter for some classes, and excessive numbers of students being sent to the office for disciplinary measures.

In the teacher's seventeenth year, a new principal was assigned, and, after reviewing the performance of the staff during the first semester, he tentatively identified the language arts teacher as one he should review more thoroughly. He visited the classroom, conferred with the language arts department coordinator, studied the teacher's official personnel file, and then telephoned the two former principals who were working in the district. They both reported that they had had many conferences with this individual during their years at the high school, some of which were written up and placed in his official file, though no corrective action had been taken. The principal was convinced that the teacher had serious problems.

Evaluations of all tenured teachers were required in March. They were to be based on the principal's personal observations, his conference with the department coordinator, and the teacher's previous history. The principal's evaluation of the language teacher cited all of the deficiencies previously referred to. The major outgrowth of the evaluation was the principal's recommendation that the teacher be terminated at the close of the school year.

The teacher's file and the principal's evaluation and recommendation were reviewed by the administrative staff and legal counsel. The principal was advised that his recommendation to terminate would not be accepted. He was further advised that he should continue to work with the teacher to improve the teacher's performance and schedule another evaluation to be held just prior to the close of the school year.

Illustrative Case—Analysis In this case, the administrative staff had recognized the teacher's problems; but in only the most severe instances were any written records kept. There was no record that the previous administrators had attempted to develop a plan of assistance for the teacher to follow in an effort to improve performance in his areas of weakness. The new principal's assessment of the teacher was substantiated by the relevant record; however, the principal's failure, and that of his predecessors, to provide the time and assistance to help the teacher overcome his weaknesses made his recommended action vulnerable and unsupportable.

Illustrative Case—Suggestions "Where do we go from here" should be a key point of discussion between the evaluator and the evaluatee as the initial follow-up to any evaluation. It is just as important for the evaluatees who are successful as it is for those adjudged as less than satisfactory. In the former instance, the follow-up may be self-initiated with encouragement and only minimal assistance from the evaluator and support staff. In the latter case, a formal written plan of assistance should be required and monitored. The evaluator should assume the responsibility for the development of the plan and should involve the evaluatee and appropriate support staff in developing it.

Supporting Documentation

Andrews, H. A. (1985).
Block, J. R. (1981).
Carroll, S. J., & Schneier, C. E. (1982).
Gorton, R. A. (1976).
McGreal, T. (1983).
McNergney, R., & Carrier, C. (1981).
Millman, J. (Ed.). (1981).
O'Dell, C. (1985).
Oliver, B. (1982).
Redfern, G. (1980).
Robertson, M. J. (1973).
Smith, H. P., & Brouwer, P. J. (1977).

FEASIBILITY STANDARDS

Summary of the Standards

F   Feasibility Standards   The Feasibility Standards call for evaluation systems that are as easy to implement as possible, efficient in their use of time and resources, adequately funded, and viable from a number of other standpoints.

F1   Practical Procedures   Personnel evaluation procedures should be planned and conducted so that they produce needed information while minimizing disruption and cost.

F2   Political Viability   The personnel evaluation system should be developed and monitored collaboratively, so that all concerned parties are constructively involved in making the system work.

F3   Fiscal Viability   Adequate time and resources should be provided for personnel evaluation activities, so that evaluation plans can be effectively and efficiently implemented.

F-1   Practical Procedures

STANDARD   Personnel evaluations should be planned and conducted so that they produce the needed information while minimizing disruption and cost.

Explanation   Personnel evaluation procedures are the series of actions that give a plan its practical effect. They should be useful to evaluators, evaluatees, and others involved in producing and receiving needed information. The steps should be specified in direct and familiar language, so that the intended evaluation process is clearly understood. The procedures should be efficient. The system should be designed to provide useful feedback without impeding the work of the institution and its staff, which is best accomplished by its being integrated into the regular operations of the organization.

Practicality is important but must not override the concern for accuracy. Above all, procedures should be chosen to produce valid information for addressing given personnel evaluation questions. They should also be consistent with the current knowledge and best practices in the personnel evaluation field. They must also comply with relevant laws and system policies. In general, the procedures should be appropriate for the information required, resources available, system goals and policies, and the recommended practices in the evaluation field.

Rationale   Impractical procedures can be inefficient and needlessly disruptive, detracting from individual performance and effectiveness and organizational efficiency. They can also impair the credibility of the institution's administration and lower staff morale. Consequently, institutions should avoid evaluation procedures that are cumbersome to implement, overly expensive, overly complex, needlessly obtrusive, and superficial.

Guidelines

A. Identify information needs, available resources, and policy requirements before designing data-collection procedures.

B. Select procedures that provide necessary information with minimal disruption.

C. Avoid duplicating information that already exists.

D. Define in familiar language all concepts or key terms of the evaluation system.

E. Define the roles of evaluators and evaluatees.

F. Help educators understand the evaluation system and its procedures through periodic orientation sessions.

G. Delineate the procedures by which evaluatees can exercise their rights to review data about their performance. (See P-2, P-4.)

H. Identify and assess published evaluation procedures as a step toward selecting or improving local procedures.

I. Review procedures periodically to assess how they could be strengthened. (See A-8.)

J. Encourage educators and others to suggest ways by which evaluation procedures can be made more useful.

Common Errors

A. Using unnecessarily complex procedures for information collection.

B. Adding or omitting procedures arbitrarily while the evaluation is in progress.

C. Disregarding complaints about evaluation procedures.

D. Unduly stressing practicality over accuracy.

Illustrative Case—Description A school district designed a plan for evaluating the instructional leadership of building principals. The plan included twenty performance categories selected by central office administrators as being important dimensions of the principal's role as an instructional leader. The categories were developed by the district's personnel director, with the help of a consultant. The evaluation plan required documentation of performance by three or more procedures for each of the twenty categories.

Once the plan was developed, four central office administrators were assigned to supervise and evaluate the principals. They were given four days of training, after which they expressed many concerns. They wondered if they understood the plan well enough to use it, had enough time to conduct all required activities, or had sufficiently clear directions regarding the use of evaluation information for personnel decision making. The principals were given a written description of the plan but not an explanation of its purposes or procedures. When the plan was implemented, a lack of time forced the omission of many procedures, so the performance dimensions actually assessed varied among the principals. As a result, the ratings given by the evaluators were not based on the same dimensions for all evaluated principals. Despite these concerns and problems, evaluator ratings were used to rank order the performance of principals as instructional leaders.

Illustrative Case—Analysis   The district's goal to enhance the performance of principals as instructional leaders was worthwhile, but the evaluation plan was complex, cumbersome, and vague. The plan included more dimensions than could be assessed and did not rank them for importance. It was time consuming and gave evaluators few rules by which to make decisions. In addition, the principals were not involved in the initial development of the plan.

Evaluators found the plan to be too complex and confusing, even after training. Moreover, the plan was unresponsive to their legitimate concerns, which, in fact, were realized during implementation.

Illustrative Case—Suggestions   A more focused plan should have been developed and communicated. Additional time and effort to train evaluators, orient evaluatees, and pilot test the plan could have been helpful. The number of dimensions evaluated and the number of procedures used to evaluate each dimension should have been reduced. Also, the principals should have been involved in planning, developing, and pilot testing the process. (See F-2.)

Supporting Documentation

Bernardin, H. J., & Beatty, R. W. (1984).
Genck, F. (1983).
Harris, B. M. (1986).

F-2 Political Viability

> **STANDARD**   The personnel evaluation system should be developed and monitored collaboratively, so that all concerned parties are constructively involved in making the system work.

Explanation   Personnel evaluation policies and procedures should provide the educator, the evaluator, and other interested parties with a common focus and set of directives concerning the goals and methods of personnel evaluation. (See P-2.) The focus and directives should be the outcome of a concerted effort by the involved parties to fashion understandable and acceptable policy and procedures. Personnel of the institution should faithfully implement the policies and procedures. Institutional decision makers should periodically review the evaluation system and revise its policies and procedures as appropriate. (See A-8.) The policies and procedures, and revisions, should be determined officially by the institution's policy board. The evaluation mandates should also be acceptable to those being evaluated, those who will contribute information to the evaluation, those who will use the results of the evaluation, and to relevant external groups. The latter would include agencies that certify educators or accredit institutions, as well as parents and selected community groups.

Rationale   If personnel evaluation policies and procedures are understandable, cooperatively developed, acceptable to all interested parties, and officially adopted, they are likely to assure continued cooperation within the personnel evaluation program. Such cooperation fosters support for the program, commitment to its purposes, acceptance of its methods, effective implementation, confidence in the reports, and trust in evaluation outcomes. In general, evaluatee support will result only if the evaluation system is officially mandated, proves to be fair, is amenable to criticism and correction, provides a due process time period for correcting deficiencies, and duly recognizes quality performance. If conditions are not politically viable, misunderstandings or disruptions are likely to occur, and those charged with carrying out evaluations are likely to be ineffectual.

Guidelines

A. Designate the policy board as the final authority in determining evaluation policies.

B. Involve instructors, department chairpersons, supervisors, administrators, evaluation specialists, policy board members, and pertinent external groups in developing personnel evaluation policies and procedures.

C. Provide sufficient time and opportunity for concerned individuals and groups to help develop, review, and revise personnel evaluation policy.

D. Institute definite procedures for obtaining regular feedback from evaluatees, evaluators, and users of the evaluations. (See A-8.)

E. Review personnel evaluation policies periodically. (See P-2.)

F. Direct special attention during the policy review process to the perspectives of evaluatees and others with legitimate interests in evaluation outcomes.

G. Rectify problems in the personnel evaluation system promptly and effectively.

Common Errors

A. Assuming that cooperation happens automatically.

B. Failing to allow sufficient time to test and install a new personnel evaluation plan.

C. Collecting but failing to address pertinent criticisms and recommendations during the policy development process.

D. Disregarding feedback provided by individuals and groups invited to review the system's overall effectiveness.

E. Failing to orient adequately new members of the organization or its external constituencies to the personnel evaluation system.

F. Attempting to evaluate the performance of an educator in the absence of official board policies on personnel evaluation.

G. Assuming that rationales, norms, or rules of tenure legally shield any educator from accountability for performance as teacher, scholar, administrator, or colleague.

H. Failing to use the "probationary" period to evaluate thoroughly a new faculty member's work before granting tenure.

I. Rushing into a merit pay plan as a public relations device without carefully determining and validating the rationale and procedures to be employed.

Illustrative Case—Description   A superintendent wanted to select staff members for promotion to administrative positions. His long-range goal was to establish an administrative academy in the district that would serve this purpose. Annually, staff members nominated as having high administrative potential would have an opportunity to attend the academy to have their administrative skills assessed and receive counseling.

The superintendent learned of a leadership workshop to be offered in a nearby city in six weeks. He saw this as an opportunity to gain firsthand information about how to establish such an academy and to start the screening process immediately.

He asked three associate superintendents to identify persons in the district who had demonstrated promise to be effective administrators. He received the names of twenty principals, supervisors, and unit directors. The superintendent next formed a screening committee, including the three associate superintendents and two assistant superintendents, which he charged to interview those of the twenty nominees who were interested and to recommend as administrative leaders the five most highly qualified individuals. The committee identified five candidates.

Several weeks after the workshop and during an administrative cabinet meeting, a letter signed by all the principals was read. The letter criticized the superintendent for failing to identify the criteria for selecting administrative leaders or providing all administrators a chance to participate in the training. The letter further criticized him for using favoritism and the "buddy system" as the basis for the selections. The principals made their points so well that the superintendent had no satisfactory response. The plan for the academy was suspended.

Illustrative Case—Analysis   While the idea of a leadership academy for new and prospective school administrators in the district may have had merit, the superintendent jeopardized its initial acceptance, and perhaps its eventual success, with hasty implementation. The superintendent was forced to be defensive, and, at that point, felt that his only choice was to ignore the concerns of the principals and proceed, or drop the idea. Since so many misunderstandings had occurred, he concluded that acceptance of the program was unlikely.

Illustrative Case—Suggestions   The superintendent should have taken timely steps to ensure the appropriate involvement of his administrative staff in this personnel evaluation action. He could have identified evaluatees, evaluators, users of the evaluations, and other pertinent groups, informed them of the purpose, and involved them in program planning, implementation, and review. He could have asked for their ideas initially, listened to their suggestions, and been as responsive as possible to their views. If he expected the system to have any permanency, he could have assured them of involvement in periodic reviews of the system. He might have constituted this group as a standing committee charged with helping to plan and periodically review the administrative academy.

Supporting Documentation

Bernardin, H. J., & Beatty, R. W. (1984).
Carroll, S. J., & Schneier, C. E. (1982).
Heneman, H. G., Schwab, D. P., Fossum, J. A., & Dyer, L. D. (1983).
Landy, F., & Farr, J. (1983).
Poliakoff, L. L. (1973).

> **STANDARD** Adequate time and resources should be provided for personnel evaluation activities, so that evaluation plans can be effectively and efficiently implemented.

Explanation Personnel evaluation systems require substantial resources to function effectively. The system must have trained evaluators, support staff, and administrative staff; the involvement of evaluatees and other individuals and groups; and on occasion the help of outside experts. Other needed resources include space, facilities, materials, equipment, and personnel time. The test of fiscal viability is whether the allocation of human and fiscal resources is sufficient to carry out the evaluation program.

Rationale The justification for expenditures for personnel evaluation may be any or all of the following: better selection of new employees, improved personnel performance, improved services to students, and improved operation and general welfare of the organization.

Resource allocation is a visible demonstration of an organization's commitment to personnel evaluation. Adequate resources provide the possibility of success; without them, an evaluation effort is prone to inappropriate compromises, shortcuts, and omissions. When limited resources impede professional, efficient evaluation practice, then evaluation data are likely to be of limited use or to have negative consequences for the organization, individuals, or both. Resource support alone, however, will not guarantee a successful evaluation program. The system must be integrated into the organization, and the information it produces must be used productively.

Guidelines

A. Define the purposes of the evaluation, how it is to be used and by whom; then make sure the resources allocated are sufficient to achieve the purposes.

B. Expend no more resources and time than necessary to obtain the needed information.

C. Estimate the personnel time required to conduct each type of personnel evaluation, and use the estimates to decide on the frequency of evaluations and to allocate staff time accordingly.

D. Calculate the funds needed to conduct the evaluation and compare this with the amount of money available for that purpose; then, if sufficient time and resources cannot be committed, modify the objectives and procedures.

E. Ensure that resources are used effectively and efficiently in the execution of the evaluation plan.

F. Maintain a search for new ideas that will help the personnel evaluation system achieve and maintain the best possible return.

Common Errors

A. Failing to allocate adequate resources to allow for evaluations of all employees in a timely, accurate, and acceptable manner.

B. Failing to allocate human and fiscal resources to develop and maintain the system.

C. Failing to allocate adequate resources to provide appropriate training of evaluators and users of the evaluations.

D. Failing to allocate adequate resources to evaluate processes used for personnel evaluation. (See A-8.)

E. Wasting resources on collecting irrelevant data.

F. Failing to follow up personnel evaluations with appropriate and effective actions or decisions. (See U-5.)

Illustrative Case—Description   In a large school district, some members of the board of education questioned the district's teacher selection procedures. They wondered if the selected candidates were highly qualified with respect to their understanding and knowledge of the subjects they would teach. After some discussion, the board approved a $1.25 million expenditure for three projects. The projects were promoted as efforts to "improve the quality of teachers in our district and the quality of what students will learn in our schools." One project employed consultants to develop a test of "necessary knowledge," which was given to all teachers and all candidates for employment. The consultants reported that almost half the teachers employed by the district were "deficient" in knowledge. The second project was an instructional skills training program, with participation mandated for all teachers. The third project, conducted by a commercial firm, involved structured interviews of all current teachers and teacher candidates. Those candidates who scored poorly were to be dismissed or rejected. Resources were not allocated to evaluate the results of these projects.

Illustrative Case—Analysis The board was willing to allocate resources to personnel evaluation and development, but did not allocate wisely. All three projects involved all teachers in the district, regardless of their existing knowledge or skills. District supervisors were not trained to use any of the project procedures. Resources were not allocated to evaluate the projects and incorporate successful procedures into a program of personnel evaluation. For these reasons, serious questions could be raised about the sound use of resources and the appropriateness of the projects selected for implementation.

Illustrative Case—Suggestions The resources available for personnel evaluation could have been spent more effectively. Alternatives could have included position analyses, a study of current staff knowledge and skills, evaluation training for administrators, and development of an articulated system for teacher selection, supervision, and development. Additionally, evaluations of current and possible selection and development plans could have been conducted. A development program could have been related to careful identification of actual skill levels and skill needs of certain teachers rather than applied uniformly and indiscriminately to all employees.

Supporting Documentation

Bacharach, S. B., Lipsky, D. B., & Shedd, J. B. (1984).
Cascio, W. F. (1982).
Genck, F. H. (1983).
Heneman, H. G., Schwab, D. P., Fossum, J. H., & Dyer, L. D. (1983).
Redfern, G. B. (1980).
Tullar, W. L., & Mullins, T. W. (1985).

Accuracy Standards

Summary of the Standards

A Accuracy Standards   The accuracy standards require that the obtained information be technically accurate and that conclusions be linked logically to the data.

A1   Defined Role   The role, responsibilities, performance objectives, and needed qualifications of the evaluatee should be clearly defined, so that the evaluator can determine valid assessment data.

A2   Work Environment   The context in which the evaluatee works should be identified, described, and recorded, so that environmental influences and constraints on performance can be considered in the evaluation.

A3   Documentation of Procedures   The evaluations procedures actually followed should be documented, so that the evaluatees and other users can assess the actual, in relation to intended, procedures.

A4   Valid Measurement   The measurement procedures should be chosen or developed and implemented on the basis of the described role and the intended use, so that the inferences concerning the evaluatee are valid and accurate.

A5   Reliable Measurement   Measurement procedures should be chosen or developed to assure reliability, so that the information obtained will provide consistent indications of the performance of the evaluatee.

A6   Systematic Data Control   The information used in the evaluation should be kept secure, and should be carefully processed and maintained, so as to ensure that the data maintained and analyzed are the same as the data collected.

A7   Bias Control   The evaluation process should provide safeguards against bias, so that the evaluatee's qualifications or performance are assessed fairly.

A8   Monitoring Evaluation Systems   The personnel evaluation system should be reviewed periodically and systematically, so that appropriate revisions can be made.

A-1 Defined Role

> **STANDARD** The role, responsibilities, performance objectives, and needed qualifications of the evaluatee should be clearly defined, so that the evaluator can determine valid assessment criteria.

Explanation All parties to the evaluation process should have the same understanding of the position requirements before the evaluation process is designed. When the position description and the person's professional activities are not in agreement, the performance expectations to be used in assessing actual job performance must be clarified. The final list of performance expectations could be derived from the tasks specified in the job description, from a review of the real professional activities, from the evaluatee's own description of the job, or from a combination of the three sources. Deliberations, in any case, should proceed in accordance with local agreements, rules, and regulations.

The role descriptions for staff members should be keyed to institutional goals and programs and reflect the best available evidence concerning the duties most crucial to staff success.

Position expectations have three parts: (1) position qualifications are the experiences, knowledge, skills, and licenses or certificates judged to be necessary to carry out the position responsibilities and fulfill the performance expectations; (2) position responsibilities are the tasks and duties performed by the person holding the position; and (3) performance objectives refer to the outcomes or results expected of the employee.

Any position expectation can be assessed at two levels. The first level is the set of general standards against which the individual's qualifications, performance, and effectiveness are to be evaluated; e.g., a teacher's college preparation to teach a certain course; his or her coverage, while teaching a course, of all the prescribed content; and the extent to which students mastered the course objectives. The second level is the set of specific performance indicators or behaviors relevant to each position standard. A classroom teacher might be asked to record and report evidence that each student satisfactorily completed classroom assignments for all class lesson plans or for the objectives in her or his individually prescribed learning plan. A researcher might be asked to record and report, for a given period, the number of published articles in refereed journals, the number of dissertations directed, and the number or dollar volume of research grants obtained.

A clear specification of the individual's role might include such factors as:

— Knowledge of the content of the job
— Effective communications
— Effective interaction with students, peers, administrators, parents, and other interested constituencies
— Participating in professional improvement activities

Rationale   This standard specifies the crucial foundation step in any personnel evaluation process. A carefully developed and sufficiently detailed and delineated description of the role, responsibilities, performance objectives, and qualifications is prerequisite to specifying relevant assessment criteria.

Guidelines

A. Develop job descriptions based on systematic job analysis.
B. Obtain position description information from as many knowledgeable sources as possible, including:

— Persons currently holding the position
— Supervisors and other decision makers
— Applicable contracts and labor agreements
— Position descriptions
— Letters of appointment

C. Define duties that reflect the needs of students, constituency, and the employing institution; e.g., teachers might explicitly be directed to:

— Demonstrate up-to-date knowledge of the curriculum and course content
— Examine and respond to the individual and collective needs of students
— Plan and deliver effective and efficient instruction, addressing the approved curriculum
— Maintain class control and good rapport with students

— Regularly assign appropriate homework and provide each student with timely feedback

— Be accessible to help individual students solve learning problems

— Regularly evaluate student progress and provide specific feedback, including reinforcement of successes and concrete steps for improvement

— Maintain clear and complete records on student participation and progress

— Maintain clear, up-to-date instructional plans to be followed by substitute teachers

— Periodically evaluate and update course content, procedures, and materials

— Maintain positive working relationships with district staff and parents

D. Specify in detail significant role behaviors, tasks, duties, responsibilities, and performance objectives.

E. Make clear the relative importance and performance level of each standard used to define success in the position.

F. Investigate and resolve any discrepancies in the position description.

G. Make clear the relationship between performance indicators and the standard with which each indicator is associated.

Common Errors

A. Excluding relevant details of the position.

B. Evaluating performance of aspects of the position that exist in written documents, such as formal position descriptions, even though they are unrelated to the actual position.

C. Specifying a position in terms of desirable traits, attitudes, and personality characteristics, rather than as tasks, duties, and needed qualifications.

D. Failing to keep a position description up-to-date and accurate.

Illustrative Case—Description A high school with a small counseling staff underwent a reduction in force and reorganization because of shrinking enrollments. A counselor who had been responsible for vocational students was then asked to take on additional responsibility for the school's college-bound students. The counselor was given a list of relevant books from which she could order as many as her budget limit would allow and was told that the books and the former college counselor's files would give her all the needed information. She used these materials to determine how she should inform students about preparing for and choosing a college. Over a six-month period with the new responsibility, she received no feedback on her work. In her evaluation, she was faulted for not reaching the college entrance rate established previously by the school district and for not having built good relations with college admissions officers.

Illustrative Case—Analysis   This case illustrates the problem of not having the role and responsibilities clearly identified. While the initial employment contract may have been detailed and clear in defining the position, the changes in responsibilities following the consolidation were vague, ambiguous, and communicated orally. The counselor saw her added role as primarily that of providing information to college-bound students. The school, though, was more concerned with maintaining a high percentage of college entrants. The school's goal, however, was never stated in writing, made a formal part of the position description, nor communicated clearly to the individual. In the absence of specified objectives, the counselor acted in accordance with her perception of her new responsibilities.

Illustrative Case—Suggestions   The added responsibility should have been more clearly incorporated into the original position description and based on a position analysis, so that the counselor could view the job as a whole, see its component parts, and understand specific tasks and expected outcomes. This would also have enabled the immediate supervisor to determine objectives and priorities and to communicate them to the counselor.

At the first sign that the counselor did not understand her new responsibilities, the supervisor should have clarified the position in discussion with the counselor, rather than postpone the clarification until the formal evaluation.

Supporting Documentation

American Psychological Association. (1980).
Bernardin, H. J., & Beatty, R. W. (1984).

Ghorpade, J., & Atchison, T. J. (1980).

Gorton, R. A. (1976).

Guion, R. M. (1961).

Heneman, H. G., Schwab, D. P., Fossum, J. A., & Dyer, L. D. (1983).

Landy, F. J., & Farr, J. L. (1980).

Medley, D. M., Coker, H., & Soar, R. S. (1984).

Pugach, M., & Rath, J. (1983).

A-2 Work Environment

STANDARD The context in which the evaluatee works should be identified, described, and recorded, so that environmental influences and constraints on performance can be considered in the evaluation.

Explanation The context in which a person works can affect performance. Among the many contextual factors that can influence or constrain performance are those associated with organizational structure and process, such as educational goals and objectives, curriculum mandates, leadership and supervisory practices, financial resources, and decision-making policies. Contextual variables also include community characteristics such as educational priorities and support, student interests and family background, and characteristics of other major clients including parents. Time, space, and instructional materials and equipment are resources that can influence performance, as can various human resources, including support services and the availability of professional expertise. Contextual factors also encompass working relations, class size, the kind and amount of discretion allowed an employee, and the professional support and contributions of colleagues. Other contextual factors that may influence performance are calamities, economic trends, social disruption, and other societal dynamics.

Conditions that are likely to affect performance should be considered so as to recognize their possible impact on performance for both the evaluator and the evaluatee. In the evaluation report, contextual factors should be referenced both to provide a fair and considered assessment of performance (see A-7) and to determine how the job description, the employee's approach, or the institution's support of the employee could be revised so as to address recurrent environmental influences better (see U-5). Contextual influences should not be used to rationalize poor performance.

Rationale Holding educators accountable for the effects of variables they cannot control or influence is likely to lead to resentment and low morale. Failure to take account of environmental factors may also threaten the validity of the evaluation process.

(See Standard A-4.) Moreover, it is in everyone's best interest for the institution to look at environmental influences in order to help employees become more effective.

On the other hand, educators must work in dynamic, complex settings, and it is part of their everyday responsibility to assess and address environmental influences. The evaluation should examine contextual factors, both to provide a fair and valid assessment of performance and accomplishments and to consider how the employee and institution might more effectively address future environmental influences. But the evaluator, the employee, and the institution must not cite contextual influences as mitigating circumstances that justify substandard service.

Guidelines

A. Identify and record contextual variables that might affect the work environment.

B. Consider available resources, working conditions, community expectations, and other context variables that might have affected performance.

Common Errors

A. Allowing environmental factors to become an excuse for poor performance.

B. Allowing contextual variables to influence the collection of data, but not its interpretation.

C. Failing to make explicit which contextual variables are being considered or disregarded.

D. Failing to state how these variables will be used for interpreting assessment data.

E. Overestimating or underestimating the influence of contextual variables when assessing performance.

Illustrative Case #1—Description   A local school board of a small school district adopted the requirement that homework be assigned each day to each class. During the evaluation process, it was noted that only the last of a particular history teacher's five classes used textbooks for homework. This observation was the basis for a negative comment on the evaluation report. The teacher questioned the evaluation, explaining that only forty texts were available for students in the five classes. Consequently, any class needing a textbook for homework other than the last class would have to return to the room to pick up books at the end of the day.

Illustrative Case #1—Analysis Under this constraint, which the teacher could not control, the negative comment was not fair or justifiable. Had contextual variables been considered, the shortage of books would have been noted and its effect on homework assignments identified.

Illustrative Case #1—Suggestions The evaluator and evaluatee could have identified, described, and recorded contextual factors prior to the evaluation and noted their possible influence on performance. It should then have been agreed how these factors would be taken into account as the evaluation was conducted.

Illustrative Case #2—Description A second grade teacher, with tenure and 15 years' experience in a large urban school district, was notorious for her inability to teach reading. Based on a succession of negative evaluations, she was transferred from an affluent neighborhood school to one in a ghetto setting. In her transfer notice, the area superintendent described her prior difficulties and deficiencies, recommended certain changes in her preparation and teaching activities, and stipulated that within two years she must obtain a satisfactory evaluation from her new building principal.

She continued to teach as before, and early in the second year of her probationary period, the school's third grade teachers complained to the principal that students coming from the class of the second grade teacher in question were far behind where they should be in reading. The principal's evaluation showed that the teacher had not implemented any of the area superintendent's recommendations, was typically unprepared and disorganized, made no attempt to address the widely varying educational levels and needs of her students, and actually spent little time in teaching reading.

In his evaluation report to the area superintendent, the principal noted that under normal circumstances he would recommend that a teacher with this record be dismissed. However, he further observed that circumstances in the neighborhood and school were so bad that whether or not a teacher taught well was inconsequential. Turnover among students averaged 90 percent annually. Absenteeism was high. Many students showed a lack of interest in education and a disrespect for school property. Students in a given class often could not speak each other's first language, and many were not fluent in English. In his report, the principal noted that someone had to baby-sit these kids and that this teacher was at least meeting this need. He thus recommended to the area superintendent that the teacher be taken off probation. He did not provide evaluative feedback and recommendations to the teacher.

Illustrative Case #2—Analysis The principal erred by ignoring the performance information because of the difficult school situation. Circumstances that influence and constrain one's ability to teach should be considered in reaching a fair evaluation, as they should be when deciding how best to improve a teacher's performance. Such circumstances must not be used as justification for accepting continuing poor service. To do so violates the intent of this standard, and also that of Service Orientation (seeing to it that we do our best to help all students learn).

Illustrative Case #2—Suggestions From the day of the transfer, the principal should have instituted ongoing formative evaluation to help the teacher take stock of her strong points, to address her demonstrated difficulties, and to improve her service in helping the children to learn. Annually, he should have conducted and reported summative evaluation. In the second year evaluation, he should have recommended termination if the teacher had not made reasonable efforts and progress, within the constraints of the setting, to improve the children's ability to read.

Supporting Documentation

Biles, B. L. (1982).
Brodinsky, B. (1984).
Emmer, E. T. et al. (1982).
Kahalas, H. (1980).
Kane, J. S., & Lawler, E. (1979).
Millman, J. (Ed.). (1981).
Morris, V. C., & Pai, Y. (1976).
Popham, W. J. (1975).
Sergiovanni, T. J. (1982).
Wiersma, W., & Gibney, T. (1985).

A-3   *Documentation of Procedures*

> **STANDARD**   The evaluation procedures actually followed should be documented, so that the evaluatees and other users can assess the actual, in relation to intended, procedures.

Explanation   The documentation should focus on the steps, forms, appeal procedures, reporting and recording schedule, follow-up, and due process procedures.

Documentation of the evaluation provides the evaluatee and other users with a clear conception of the evidence gathered and the procedures followed.

Rationale   The effectiveness of an evaluation is linked to how well the evaluator, evaluatee, and other appropriate persons understand and accept the evaluation procedures. A uniform, systematic, carefully documented method of evaluation helps to ensure that the evaluation system will be equitable, fair, and legal.

Poor designs or poor implementation of sound designs can produce erroneous results. All appropriate personnel should be helped to understand and invited to evaluate the design and the actual process.

Guidelines

A. Monitor evaluations and maintain appropriate records of their timing and steps, making special note of any important deviations from the institution's approved evaluation system. (See P-2 and A-8.)

B. Provide all evaluatees and other users with feedback forms on which to criticize or suggest improvements in the evaluation system. (See F-2 and A-8.)

C. Periodically provide all employees with orientation and training in the evaluation process. (See P-2.)

Common Errors

A. Making an evaluation plan so inflexible that unanticipated events cannot be accommodated.

B. Failing to document exceptions to the design procedure.

Illustrative Case—Description   The dean of a community college expressed concern to the head of one department about continuing complaints regarding one instructor.

The department head made a preliminary, informal investigation by observing one of the instructor's classes and by talking privately with a few instructors and students. He got very consistent and convincing information and concluded that the instructor was indeed doing a poor job. This conclusion seemed so obvious that the head decided to forgo formal evaluation and documentation. He made no written record of the evaluation and did not inform the dean of his procedures, findings, or intended next steps.

Instead, he immediately met privately with the instructor and communicated his conclusions orally to the instructor, pointing out the "wasted minutes" during the class period, the instructor's apparent ignorance of his students' abilities, his habit of communicating to students that he held low expectations of their performances, his penchant for intimidating and embarrassing them, and his failure to return graded assignments or provide students with feedback on their work.

The instructor agreed that he needed to improve in these areas. He also complimented the head on being so perceptive and learning so much about his shortcomings so quickly. He did not contest any of the head's conclusions and did not request a written report. The head advised the instructor to do better.

Six months later, the head made an unscheduled visit to the instructor's classroom. After a half hour, the head concluded that there had been no improvement. When they met later to discuss the observation, the instructor conceded that his teaching was poor and wasn't getting better. Consequently, the department head informed the instructor that his contract would not be renewed the following year. The verbal notice was followed up with a written confirmation.

The instructor immediately began seeking other employment, but couldn't find a job. He decided he shouldn't have accepted the dismissal notice and consulted with the faculty member officially in charge of faculty grievances.

Upon reviewing the case, the faculty representative told the instructor, the department head, and the dean that the instructor did not have to accept the dismissal. The department head had failed to use the forms and procedures specified in the college's official evaluation plan. It didn't matter that the instructor had agreed with the evaluations; an appropriate written record of the evaluation was not available for use in defense of the decision. The only written record contained only the conclusions; it did not describe the procedures followed or present the evidence obtained. There was little doubt that the instructor could successfully appeal the ruling.

The dean agreed with the analysis, and the department head reluctantly withdrew the letter of dismissal. The instructor welcomed the financial security provided by his continued contract. In private, he agreed that his performance was poor and that the evaluation had been just, fair, and accurate. However, he said he couldn't afford to give up the position.

Illustrative Case—Analysis   The termination decision was justified in the minds of the department head, the dean, and even the instructor. The evaluations were viewed as fair and appropriate. Nevertheless, because specified procedures had not been followed or recorded, the evaluation could not be used to support a dismissal decision. The department head failed to specify the consequences of poor performance as required in the evaluation plan and did not record the steps followed in gathering data and providing feedback.

Illustrative Case—Suggestions   The dean should have reminded the department head of the requirements of the approved college plan for personnel evaluations. The head should have followed and maintained records of the prescribed steps and of the obtained information. The officials of the institution should have evaluated and improved the evaluation system to ensure that it could result in just dismissals.

Supporting Documentation

American Psychological Association. (1980).
Barber, T. X. (1976).

Bernardin, H. J., & Beatty, R. W. (1984).
Gorton, R. A. (1976).
Henderson, R. (1981).
Medley, D. M., Coker, H., & Soar, R. S. (1984).
Patten, T. H., Jr. (1982).

A-4   Valid Measurement

> **STANDARD** The measurement procedures should be chosen or developed and implemented on the basis of the described role and the intended use, so that the inferences concerning the evaluatee are valid and accurate.

Explanation Evidence for the validity of an evaluation procedure must be assembled and available.

Valid means that what was intended to be measured was measured. Specifically here, valid refers to the degree to which evidence supports the inferences that are drawn from the measurement instruments or procedures. Valid does not refer to the instruments or procedures themselves. Thus, a particular measure may be valid for one purpose but have little or no validity for another purpose.

It is intended in this standard that the term "measurement" be used in its broadest sense—any instrument or procedure used to collect information that will form the basis for evaluating an individual's qualifications, performance, or effectiveness.

Decisions about what to measure in a personnel evaluation should be guided by careful attention to standards U-2 Described Use and A-1 Described Role.

The various strategies for presenting evidence of validity include correctly inferring a trait or characteristic (for example, verbal ability) from empirical evidence; correctly inferring a relationship between an assessed characteristic used to predict a level of performance and the observed future performance; and presenting the self-evident relationship between the content of a measurement device or procedure and performance, where the measurement content includes a representative sample of the job tasks involved.

The issues, standards, guidelines, and technical details of the validation process are treated in detail elsewhere (AERA/APA/NCME, 1985; APA, Division 14, 1980). Therefore, those details are not repeated here. Those who are responsible for assessing the validity of any particular educational personnel evaluation procedure are advised to take into account the extensive discussions of validity in those two documents.

Rationale   Validity is the single most important issue in the assessment of any evaluation process. If the evaluation is to serve its intended purpose, then the inferences and judgments that are made must be defensible. The selection, development, and implementation of the instruments and procedures for collecting information, as well as the basis for synthesizing the information and drawing inferences from it, must be clearly linked to the purposes for which judgments, inferences, and decisions are made. Further, these linkages must be documented and made public. (See A-3.)

Guidelines

A. Establish criteria for selecting and developing measurement procedures based on the proposed use of the evaluation and the involved role. (See U-2, P-2, and A-3.) Such criteria might include:

— Collecting multiple assessments of instruction to ensure that the data obtained are of sufficient depth and breadth.

— Assessing accomplishments (output) against a careful description of what the job is to accomplish.

B. Ensure that plans for full implementation of the measurement procedures are based on a careful review of the intended uses. (See U-2.)

C. Involve those who are to be affected by the system in determining its purposes, processes, assessment criteria, and instruments, and in assessing its validity. (See F-2 and P-3.)

D. Conduct unscheduled observations as a check on data obtained from scheduled observations.

E. In observing teaching or other performance, use structured, objectively recorded observation schedules as a check on techniques that allow recording only summary judgments based on what was perceived.

F. Field test the measurement procedures using appropriate validation techniques.

G. Ensure the validity of any measurement procedures that disproportionately affect members of any identifiable subgroup. (See A-7.)

H. Make the results of the validation process public and describe the results in terms that are understandable and meaningful to evaluatees and other interested individuals and groups. (See A-8.)

I. Report validity results openly and completely and include descriptions of what inferences are supported by validity evidence and what precautions must be taken in using them for decision making. (See A-8.)

J. Encourage sufficient flexibility in negotiated contracts, legislation, and board policy so that evaluation instrumentation and measurement procedures can be improved to enhance validity over time.

Common Errors

A. Concentrating on the parts of the job that are easiest to assess.

B. Failing to confirm or reject alleged strengths or weaknesses of an individual through observing and documenting performance and discussing it with the employee.

C. Using a measurement procedure for multiple purposes when it is valid for only one, e.g., using students' scores on a nationally standardized test to assess the performance of a teacher or administrator when the test has not been validated for the latter purpose.

D. Failing to include information that has been identified as relevant to the evaluation purpose (deficiency).

E. Including in an evaluation measures or other information with no demonstrated relevance to the purpose of the evaluation, e.g., including information because it is readily available or easily obtained rather than because it is relevant (contamination).

F. Assuming that a procedure is valid solely because it "seems reasonable" or is common practice.

G. Failing to take account of factors over which the evaluatee has no control. (See A-2.)

H. Failing to document the validation process.

Illustrative Case #1—Description Faculty evaluations in a large, urban elementary school are conducted by the school principal. Each teacher's class is visited five times during the year by the principal. After the visit, the principal completes a one-page evaluation form that provides ratings on classroom control, skill in presentation, teaching style, and overall effectiveness.

A copy of the completed form is shared with the teacher. Near the end of the year, the principal meets with each teacher to examine and discuss trends, consistencies, and inconsistencies in the results of the five observations.

Illustrative Case #1—Analysis Issues of reliability of the observation data are addressed by making five observations. Also, the evaluation procedure appropriately calls for making the results of the observation data available to the teacher. Provision for discussion of the five sets of results at the end of the year may help to correct other deficiencies in the evaluation.

Nevertheless, evaluation appears to be based on a very narrow and limited sample of information. Observation of a teacher's classroom performance is only one of many important means for assessing a teacher's effectiveness. Moreover, the variables included in the observation schedule do not address such important issues as the quantity and quality of content the teacher expects students to learn or the effects of instruction on student attitudes and achievements.

Illustrative Case #1—Suggestions Teacher evaluations must assess not only the pedagogical skills of the teacher but also the quality of the curriculum the teacher provides to students. The principal should examine a sample of the teacher's instructional materials, and, as the need arises, should obtain independent assessments from a supervisor, master teacher, curriculum expert, or other specialist.

Also, assessment of classroom procedures should be augmented by assessing the extent that student needs are being met. The teacher might be asked to assess and document individual and collective needs of the students at the beginning of the year and, periodically thereafter, to assess and document individual and collective progress related to the assessed needs.

Illustrative Case #2—Description A school district implemented a plan to evaluate all its building principals, a large percentage of whom had been in their positions for more than twenty years. The board of education mandated the evaluation to determine the principals' needs for professional development and planned to use the results, in collaboration with the superintendent, to fund training sessions and grant study leaves.

The superintendent employed a consultant to develop an evaluation system involving observations and interviews. The consultant established criteria for determining minimum competency for the position of principal and then constructed instruments and standards to assess the criteria. As a result of the ensuing evaluation, several principals were judged below the minimum competency level.

The superintendent recommended to the board of education that these principals be removed from their positions. The board rejected the recommendation and reprimanded the superintendent for ignoring their instructions.

Illustrative Case #2—Analysis The superintendent's initial validity error was in not communicating to the consultant the board's intention to use the results to help the principals improve their performance; his second mistake was in using the information for a purpose other than the one for which it had been commissioned. The consultant erred by assuming without checking that the instruments and procedures should be valid for determining minimal competence and not establishing that they should be valid for planning a professional development program. The board met the intent of this standard by keeping to the intended use of the information and rejecting information not addressed to this use.

Illustrative Case #2—Suggestions The superintendent should have reached a written agreement with the board concerning the intended use of the evaluation. The agreement should have been shared with the consultant and the principals. The superintendent and the board should have held the consultant to meeting the requirements of the written agreement, and they should have been faithful in meeting it themselves.

Supporting Documentation

American Psychological Association. (1980).
American Psychological Association. (1985).
Bernardin, H. J., & Beatty, R. W. (1984).
Brophy, J., & Good, T. L. (1986).
Carroll, S. J., & Schneier, C. E. (1982).
Coker, H., Medley, D., & Soar, R. (1980).
Jacobs, R., Kafry, D., & Zedreck, S. (1980).
Landy, F. J., & Farr, J. L. (1983).
Medley, D. M., Coker, H., & Soar, R. S. (1984).
Millman, J. (Ed.). (1981).

Smith, P. C. (1976).
Soar, R. S., Medley, D. M., & Coker, H. (1983).
Thorndike, R. L., & Hagen, E. (1977).
Wise, A., Darling-Hammond, L., McLaughlin, M., & Bernstein, H. (1984).

A-5 Reliable Measurement

> **STANDARD** Measurement procedures should be chosen or developed and implemented to assure reliability, so that the information obtained will provide consistent indications of the performance of the evaluatee.

Explanation A reliable measure is one that provides consistent information about the performance being assessed (AERA/APA/NCME, 1985).

Any data-gathering procedure or instrument will be subject to sources of error that may cause inconsistencies in the measurement of a single characteristic. Inconsistencies may exist in (a) the way an evaluatee responds to the same set of test items or performs on different occasions, (b) the way in which an observer interprets the same elements of behavior on different occasions, or (c) the way in which several observers will rate the same sample of evaluatee performance on a given occasion.

Consistency should be sought across different indicators of the same criterion (internal consistency), across different observers of the same behavior (observer agreement), and across different occasions on which a behavior is observed (stability).

The steps to secure acceptable reliability and the level of reliability realized should be documented and made known to interested parties. (See A-8.)

Rationale Individual personnel evaluation instruments and the procedures used should have levels of reliability that are acceptable for intended uses. Procedures that lack reliability will also lack validity. The affected persons have a right to know what efforts were made to enhance reliability and the reliability levels achieved.

Guidelines

A. Acquire evidence for all types of reliability that are relevant to the intended uses of the instrument before using it in personnel evaluation.

B. Check for inconsistency in interpretations of measurement results.

C. Estimate and report reliability of instruments for the particular situation.

D. Train observers to apply the rating criteria consistently and objectively.

E. Train the evaluators to use procedures and instruments correctly.

F. In developing instruments, take into account research that has identified internally consistent dimensions of pertinent behavior.

G. Employ multiple measures, multiple observers, and multiple occasions for data collection as appropriate to minimize inconsistency and discern consistent patterns and trends.

Common Errors

A. Confusing reliability with validity. Reliability is a necessary, but not a sufficient, condition for validity. (See A-4.)

B. Assuming that the reliability of a procedure is the same for different groups and situations.

C. Assuming that published reliability estimates are necessarily applicable to the intended use.

D. Failing to consider that unusual circumstances may have influenced the evaluatee's behavior.

E. Failing to assess the reliability of a pilot instrument before using it to make judgments about a person's performance.

Illustrative Case #1—Description An assistant professor of political science was being considered for promotion and tenure at a university. He was developing expertise in computer applications to research and teaching in public administration.

His university's primary basis for promotion and tenure was research and publication. In line with department requirements, the assistant professor submitted his list of publications for evaluation. A small number of articles were published in established, mainline journals in political science; the bulk of the papers were in journals specializing in computer applications. One of these journals dealt with various fields including public administration; the other was specifically focused on computer applications and did not apply to any specific field.

The senior faculty responsible for conducting the evaluation rejected the assistant professor's application for promotion and tenure. They reported that they had had neither the time nor interest to study his articles on computer applications, that they weren't familiar with the journals in which they were published, and that they doubted that these articles were of much significance to the field of political science. They speculated that any political scientist who published in such off-beat journals was suspect of being a dilettante.

Shortly after the decision of the senior faculty, a number of the assistant professor's papers were cited in a highly laudatory way by two of the most prominent political scientists in Public Administration. Subsequently, the same professors who had ruled against promotion and tenure for the assistant professor studied his articles, cited them in some of their own publications, and privately admitted to the dean that they had been hasty and incorrect in their prior judgments of the articles.

Illustrative Case #1—Analysis   The senior faculty in this case made judgments concerning an area of scholarship about which they were not well informed. Initially, they made only a superficial study of the computer publications and did not investigate the quality of the two computer-oriented journals. As a consequence, they made a collective judgment that disagreed with the judgment of experts in the field and with their own subsequent assessments.

Illustrative Case #1—Suggestions   The senior faculty should have thoroughly informed themselves about the assistant professor's publications before reaching a conclusion about their merit and worth. They should have studied the materials, and might also have submitted the articles, along with the applicant's publication list, to qualified experts. Also, they should have investigated the reputation of the two journals about which they were not informed.

Illustrative Case #2—Description   Faculty evaluations in a middle school are conducted by the vice principal. Among other data collection methods, each teacher's class is visited once during the year by the vice principal. After the visit, the principal completes a two-page form that provides ratings on classroom management, time devoted to learning tasks, skill in presentation, engagement of all students in the learning process, feedback to students, clarity of assignments, and overall effectiveness. A copy of the completed form is shared with the teacher.

Illustrative Case #2—Analysis The classroom observation procedure used in this school suffers from inadequate information about the quality of the teachers' work. A single occasion of observation is insufficient because the information is not likely to be representative. For example, the occasion might be one when the students are excited or upset because of some unusual event in the classroom or school. Data collected on such an occasion is questionable.

It is to be noted that this case parallels case #1 under Standard A-4 Valid Measurement. In the former case, a lack of validity was noted due to a narrow range of criteria and only one data collection technique, but reliability of the information collected was adequately addressed due to repeated classroom observations, standard observation procedures, and demonstration of consistent findings. In the present case, validity was enhanced by employing a wide range of criteria and multiple measures, but one of the measures, classroom observation, was shown to have questionable reliability.

Illustrative Case #2—Suggestions There is no ideal number of observations required to arrive at or assess reliability of findings. The important point is that a pattern or trend in the data must be clearly established for the data to be useful and defensible. Cases where other information casts uncertainty on the teachers' competence may require more classroom observations than those whose results are consistent across the various evaluation procedures. A good rule of thumb is to conduct additional observations at appropriate intervals until it is evident that no new, important information is being obtained. The school in this example might conduct an exploratory study of a sample of teachers observed ten times during a school year to determine the point where additional observations do not provide new information.

Supporting Documentation

AERA/APA/NCME. (1985).
Bartko, J. J. (1976).
Cooper, W. H. (1981).
Frick, T., & Semmel, M. I. (1978).

McGaw, G., Wardrop, J. L., & Bunda, M. A. (1972).
Medley, D., Coker, H., & Soar, R. S. (1984).
Millman, J. (Ed.). (1981).
Rowley, G. L. (1976).

A-6 Systematic Data Control

> **STANDARD** The information used in the evaluation should be kept secure, and should be carefully processed and maintained, so as to ensure that the data maintained and analyzed are the same as the data collected.

Explanation Information should be carefully processed and checked for accuracy at every stage of collection, storage, and retrieval. Accuracy checks should be made of recorded data, data entered into storage, data retrieved from files, and data entered into analysis.

The integrity of the information base should be protected by careful maintenance and security. The data and supporting documentation should be kept confidential, and careful oversight exercised regarding their access and retrieval. (See P-4.)

Rationale Personnel decisions resulting from evaluations can be no better than the information upon which they are based. Systematic data control minimizes the errors introduced into the information base. Evaluators have limited control over such matters as sampling and measurement errors, but they have considerably more control over scoring, coding, data entry, and analysis, and they can play an important part in minimizing errors in these areas. If undetected, such errors can distort the results of the data analysis and render the evaluation inaccurate and misleading. Also, indiscriminate sharing of evaluation findings can discredit the evaluation system.

Guidelines

A. Establish policies and procedures to control who has access to information collected for personnel evaluation. (See P-2 and P-4.)

B. Select those who type or handle personnel evaluation materials, require that they maintain strict confidentiality, and train them to do so. (See P-4.)

C. Ensure that people included in processing the information have the necessary training and background to perform their tasks accurately.

D. Ensure that the people involved in the actual coding of the data are familiar with and understand the criteria, context, and other components of the evaluation.

E. Spot check by recording and comparing the results.

F. Identify files or entries by individual and group characteristics, so there will be no doubt about what information is associated with whom. This is especially important for supporting documents.

G. Write a date and reason for data collection on each entry, so that files may be easily updated or used for longitudinal data analysis, and not used for unintended or inappropriate purposes.

H. Provide employees an opportunity to enter explanations, clarifications, or objections to particular evaluation findings when they are entered into their personnel files. (See P-4.)

I. Require employees to sign each evaluation report placed in their file, indicating that they have seen the report and had an opportunity to discuss it. (See P-4.)

J. Prepare duplicate data sets and keep a back-up set in a secure location. This is especially important when there is a chance that fire, theft, computer malfunctions, data processing error, or staff neglect can cause vital information to be lost.

K. Label evaluation documents as ORIGINAL or COPY.

L. Develop a filing system for information, so that it can be easily and accurately retrieved when needed.

M. Maintain complete and well-documented records on all evaluation follow-up. (See P-1 and P-2.)

N. Maintain files for a reasonable amount of time.

O. Assure the integrity of information removed from the office or storage location.

Common Errors

A. Failing to include and follow procedures for checking the accuracy of data recording, coding, storage, and retrieval in any personnel evaluation plan.

B. Failing to maintain an "audit trail" for the data.

C. Failing to keep back-up information up-to-date.

Illustrative Case #1—Description The superintendent of a middle-sized school district asked the personnel director to establish a personnel evaluation system for all employees of the district including the superintendent. Certain standard information, such as highest earned degree, was to be collected on each person and then updated annually. In addition, evaluative information would be added each year for each employee.

The personnel director decided to put all information on the school district's hard disk storage. One year and $50,000 worth of staff time and support services were spent collecting, preparing, and storing the data. It was a one-time investment.

At the end of the year, the superintendent requested a listing of all personnel and their evaluation ratings over the past two years. The superintendent planned to use the information for inservice training programs for those personnel rated unsatisfactory. When the listing arrived, the superintendent discovered that those personnel rated high one year were rated extremely low the next year, and vice versa. There was no consistency across years. He sought an explanation from the personnel director, who, after much investigation, discovered that the person coding the evaluation data the previous year had erroneously reversed the numbers of the rating scale, and thus had reversed the true ratings.

Illustrative Case #1—Analysis   The use of a computerized data base provided the district with a means for systematic data control. However, there was a failure to audit the data for human error.

He should have provided for verifying the accuracy of the data prior to entry into the system. In addition, the personnel director should have provided an orientation and training session to all employees responsible for coding personnel data.

This case demonstrates the potential for significant harm when personnel decisions are based on distorted, erroneous evaluation data.

Illustrative Case #1—Suggestions   Many things can go wrong in the area of systematic data control. Careful and detailed planning, and checkpoints throughout the collection, recording, and analysis of data, must be in place prior to implementing data control procedures.

Illustrative Case #2—Description   The superintendent of a school district asked the school principals to help him select a social studies teacher to receive an award for meritorious performance. The award was a gift from a member of the community and was to be given only once. The recipient of the award was to have proven leadership ability and a strong performance record.

The principals carefully studied their employees' records and previous performance evaluations. They submitted their nominations, along with explanations, rationales, and back-up documentation. The superintendent had his secretary compile the reports into a common file. Then he and the principals convened to evaluate the nominations and select a winner. After the decision was reached, the superintendent disposed of the file.

The committee notified the winner that she would receive the award, scheduled an awards dinner, and sent news releases to the major newspapers in the area. Two weeks later, three social studies teachers, who felt that they should have received the award, filed grievances. Two of these grievances were handled with relative ease. The third was submitted by the individual who had been runner-up in the award competition. The committee reconvened and discussed their decision, which reaffirmed their confidence in their decision and evaluation procedures.

The disgruntled individual followed the grievance process through the various stages. Finally, with no other options available, the individual requested that an arbitrator settle the dispute. Both parties had three weeks to put their case together for presentation to the arbitrator.

The principals and the superintendent met to review the case, but, having disposed of the file of information, they were unable to reconstruct the evaluation data or to defend their decision.

Illustrative Case #2—Analysis   Personnel evaluations always carry the potential for error. Evaluators must respect the right of evaluatees to have evaluations reviewed and justified. They must protect the integrity of their evaluations by maintaining complete files for a reasonable length of time. In this case, the files should have been kept at least until after the award was given, and, to be safe, for a year after that. The consequences of the errors in this instance demonstrate the prudence of that practice, for ad hoc as well as annual evaluations.

Illustrative Case #2—Suggestions   The Superintendent could have taken responsibility for maintaining the award competition file. He could have designated a filing cabinet in his office for that purpose and assigned his secretary to maintain the file and control access to it. He could have specified that the file be maintained for a reasonable length of time, such as one year.

Supporting Documentation

American Association of School Personnel Administrators. (1978).
Anderson, S., Bell, S., Murphy, R. T., & associates. (1975).
Bolton, D. L. (1973).
Castetter, W. B. (1981).
Wexley, K. N., & Yuki, G. A. (1984).

A-7 Bias Control

> **STANDARD** The evaluation process should provide safeguards against bias, so that the evaluatee's qualifications or performance are assessed fairly.

Explanation There is constant potential for the intrusion of bias in personnel evaluations. Evaluations are biased if judgments are reached partially or totally on considerations irrelevant to the job. An unbiased evaluation is one which is based solely on criteria and information relevant to the evaluatee's job. (See A-1 and A-5.)

Rationale The presence of bias can entirely undermine an evaluation system. Bias can distort the information-gathering process and corrupt decisions, actions, and recommendations. Bias can also lead to expensive and damaging court cases.

Guidelines

A. Involve evaluatees and other pertinent personnel in designing the evaluation process. (See U-1 and F-2.)

B. Train evaluators, evaluatees, and others in the use of the evaluation system. (See U-3.)

C. Provide ample, timely opportunities for criticizing the evaluation system. (See A-8.)

D. Exclude factors from the process that disadvantage some evaluatees despite their actual performance level; e.g., a prerequisite period of experience or seniority that rules out candidates who otherwise are highly qualified. (See A-4.)

E. Obtain data and judgments from multiple sources and preserve the independent data and judgments for the possibility of independent review. (See A-4 and A-8.)

F. Allow evaluatees and other relevant personnel ample opportunity to review data and participate in interpreting it. (See U-4 and U-5.)

G. Compare the results of unscheduled observations with those from scheduled observations. (See A-4 and A-5.)

H. Be particularly alert to the potential for bias in those parts of the evaluation system that are more subjective than objective. (See A-4 and A-5.)

I. Provide for prompt, third party reviews of appeals.

Common Errors

A. Continuing to use evaluators whose biases have become evident. (See P-3.)

B. Allowing the evaluation process to focus on aspects of performance or personal projects irrelevant to identified roles.

C. Judging qualifications or performance on the basis of irrelevant characteristics such as race, age, sex, or religion, or other characteristics that are not job related. (See A-4.)

D. Ignoring or distorting certain relevant information because it conflicts with the general conclusion or recommendation.

E. Basing a conclusion on outdated information about an educator's performance. (See A-4.)

Illustrative Case—Description   A new principal in a local high school wanted to reassign the biology teacher to teach home economics. Though the teacher, a woman, was certified to teach both subjects, the principal thought that biology was more appropriately the domain of men. He also believed that too many female students were receiving A's in biology and suspected the teacher of giving preferential treatment.

The principal observed the teacher's biology classes for two consecutive days and rated her performance unsatisfactory. He told the teacher that her lecture method was inadequate for proficient instruction. He suggested that she begin her lectures with overviews, proceed with direct instruction, and end with more opportunity for student questions and discussion.

He observed her teaching again two weeks later, and concluded that she had not improved her lectures. He rated her performance unsatisfactory and reassigned her to teach home economics.

Illustrative Case—Analysis   Bias entered this evaluation process at several points and persisted unchecked. The principal believed that women are intellectually weaker than men and that certain subjects are the exclusive domain of one sex or the other.

These prejudices may well have induced his conclusion that the teacher gave her female students preferential treatment. The principal made no apparent effort to check his premises, either before or during the evaluation process. He conducted the evaluation himself, did so very narrowly and unprofessionally, obtained no independent assessment, and provided no opportunity for appeal.

The sole data collection method was classroom observation, and no opportunity was provided for discussion between the teacher and evaluator. Others who might be sources of valid and reliable information about the teacher were not consulted. School documents and records, such as student grades, earlier evaluations, or parent communications, went unexamined. Furthermore, the classroom observation itself was not checked for technical adequacy.

This evaluation produced no convincing evidence that the teacher was ineffective in teaching biology.

Illustrative Case—Suggestions   The evaluation system should have protected teachers against the use of evaluation as a pretext for confirming previously made decisions. It should also have provided for an appeal of evaluations and review by an independent agent.

If the evaluation were to proceed, it should have been conducted by someone acceptable to both the teacher and the principal. The purpose of the evaluation should have been clarified and justified. The evaluation should have been keyed to the relevant job descriptions and employed multiple sources of relevant data. It should have been checked for technical adequacy. Finally, the principal should have engaged the teacher in a discussion to reach a sound, unbiased decision.

Supporting Documentation

Carroll, S. J., & Schneier, C. E. (1982).
Fletcher, C. (1984).
Gorton, R. A. (1976).
Henderson, R. (1981).
Imundo, L. V. (1980).
Kaye, B. L. (1982).
Manasse, A. L. (1984).

A-8 Monitoring Evaluation Systems

> **STANDARD** The personnel evaluation system should be reviewed periodically and systematically, so that appropriate revisions can be made.

Explanation Personnel evaluation involves purposes, procedures, instruments, reports, and uses of findings. Each of these components and the system as a whole should be evaluated at regular intervals, preferably annually, and when complaints or problems surface.

Reviews should be based on the extent to which the evaluation system is being implemented as planned, the extent to which it is achieving its purposes, and the extent to which it is accepted by evaluatees and other stakeholders. The reviews should, in general, consider if the standards in this document are being addressed and met.

If the evaluation system is not being implemented across units as planned, appropriate staff development activities or personnel adjustments must be enacted. If the evaluation system is not achieving the purposes for which it was designed, the system should be examined and modified appropriately, or the initial expectations concerning those purposes should be revised.

The results of the reviews should be used to strengthen problem areas and thus increase the effectiveness and fairness of the evaluation system. If a review indicates that changes are necessary, the same concerns for utility, feasibility, propriety, and accuracy will apply to the revised system.

Rationale Personnel evaluation is difficult to do well and is subject to mistakes and complaints. It is also subject to modification to keep pace with developments in the evaluation field. Accordingly, even when personnel evaluation systems seem to be working satisfactorily, they should be kept in a state of review, evolution, and improvement.

Even a well-planned system cannot be implemented successfully without evaluators and evaluatees identifying some problems or concerns. In addition, it must be recognized that individuals and their working conditions change, which necessitates a regular review of evaluation procedures.

It is also important to investigate complaints to ensure fairness, to avoid expensive appeals and litigation, and to identify components of the system that need to be revised.

Guidelines

A. Investigate whether the evaluation system is having a positive effect on the quantity and quality of educational outputs.

B. Budget sufficient resources and personnel time to review the evaluation process regularly. (See F-3.)

C. Identify the parts of the evaluation system that require more frequent review or close monitoring.

D. Compare actual specific evaluation tasks with the evaluation plan.

E. Periodically survey the staff to obtain their criticisms and recommendations.

F. Engage a representative group to review and revise at least annually personnel evaluation policies and procedures.

G. Review the evaluation policies and plans against the standards in this document and other relevant sources.

H. Train evaluatees, evaluators, and others in using these standards to evaluate the evaluation system.

I. Check that the validity and reliability information is current and adequate. (See A-4 and A-5.)

Common Errors

A. Assuming that a well-developed and carefully implemented performance evaluation system will continue to operate as well in succeeding years as it does the first year.

B. Failing to train agency staff for their roles in personnel evaluation beyond the initiation year of a personnel evaluation system.

C. Failing to monitor and record the extent to which evaluations fulfill due process requirements.

D. Failing to determine if the evaluation system is having positive effects on the quality of educational outputs.

E. Revising the evaluation system without consulting the users.

Illustrative Case #1—Description   A school system received federal funds to develop a performance-based teacher evaluation system. A representative steering committee of teachers, administrators, and teacher organization representatives was formed to oversee the development of the system. Considerable time and effort were devoted to planning the system. Each component was pilot tested and then refined. Inservice training was provided for teachers and administrators during the year preceding its implementation. Then the evaluation system was put into effect, with principals assuming responsibility for the process.

Three years later, the teachers' association of the school district began receiving an unusual number of complaints from teachers in five of the schools. The basic concern was that principals in these schools were making fewer and fewer classroom observation visits, and there were cases in which evaluations were conducted based on a single visit. After several unsatisfactory sessions with the superintendent, the teachers' association complained strongly to the school board, which, now, five years after the evaluation system was first implemented, instructed the superintendent to review the evaluation system.

Illustrative Case #1—Analysis This well-planned teacher evaluation system was initially implemented quite well. As often occurs, however, over time some of those responsible for making evaluations became lax and began taking "shortcuts." Although principals were responsible for evaluating their professional staff, evaluation was only one of their many duties, and not one they enjoyed. Since their evaluations were not monitored, the principals were able to depart significantly from the prescribed procedures, and some of them had done so.

Illustrative Case #1—Suggestions The superintendent in this system could have instituted a strictly enforced policy of checking (twice a year, for example) that each principal was making *at least* the specified minimum number of classroom observation visits. If this frequent, but relatively easily accomplished, monitoring indicated consistent patterns of non-compliance, the superintendent would have been in a position to take immediate steps to correct the problem. These might have included periodic retraining of principals in the use of the system, a comprehensive review of the entire evaluation system, and the usual appropriate corrective actions directed at the non-complying principals.

Illustrative Case #2—Description The dean of the College of Education at a large state-supported university appointed a faculty committee to make recommendations for a procedure for admission into the undergraduate teacher education program. The faculty appointed to the committee represented each department in the College of Education.

The dean charged the committee to recommend a basic skills test for inclusion in the admissions process, and to propose a procedure for validating its use in the program.

The committee concentrated on selecting the basic skills test, and talked little about other techniques and procedures for making admissions decisions.

After spending considerable time, the committee found that there were no commercial tests that satisfied their content specifications for the basic skills test. As time was running short in the semester, and a decision had to be made, the committee nevertheless recommended an available test. They reported that it covered the three required areas of reading, math, and writing, was reasonably priced, and was accompanied by an administration and scoring service. Unfortunately, the test did not meet the committee's test content specifications.

They recommended to the dean that students who wished to be admitted into the teacher education program should be required to submit the following before the end of their sophomore year in the university:

— An application form with personal information, an essay on why they wished to become a teacher, and grades from their completed college courses
— Their scores on the basic skills test
— Three letters of recommendation

They also recommended a pilot year of using the basic skills test, so that student performance could be examined and realistic cut-scores set. The committee was also concerned about the potential for gender and race bias inherent in the use of the test, and recommended that scores be examined as a safeguard against it.

Illustrative Case #2—Analysis   This entry into the teaching profession personnel evaluation system was sketchy in its design and hence a good candidate for careful monitoring and further development. It needed to be reviewed and pilot tested. It was wise of the committee to recommend a pilot year, because the purpose of the design left many decisions to be made. A careful analysis of the design using *The Personnel Evaluation Standards* prior to, and during, the pilot year would have guided the committee toward a more complete and defensible plan.

The committee also could have used the *Standards for Educational and Psychological Tests* (APA, 1985) to guide their choice of tests, and to assess their selection during the pilot year. If the test proved to have serious flaws, they could and should have considered alternatives.

Illustrative Case #2—Suggestions   Once an admissions procedure is fully designed, the committee would want to involve all concerned groups in a review of the system and the results of the pilot test. By opening the system to public review, the committee would be demonstrating its openness to revising the procedure before implementation. If major issues emerged, the committee might want to delay implementation another year until the flaws were corrected and agreement achieved.

Once the system was implemented, the dean might want to assign an individual or a committee to conduct an annual review. They could examine the quality and demographics of candidates admitted and those denied with the system in effect. They could use *The Personnel Evaluation Standards* to guide their reviews. They might give special attention to contextual changes that could require revision of the system with regard to costs and benefits, fairness in providing minorities with access to teacher education, validity and reliability of measurements, administrative complexity, uniformity of use, and ease of central control.

Supporting Documentation

Bolton, D. L. (1980).
Doyle, K. O. (1983).
Iwanicki, E. F. (1982).
Oliver, B. (1982).
Sergiovanni, T. J. (1984).

PART 2

Applying the Standards

In the preceding part of this book, each of the 21 standards was accompanied by one or more illustrative cases to show how the standard could be applied to assess and improve particular evaluations. Thus, the reader was given guidance for applying each standard. This part looks at the standards as a group and its purpose is to provide guidance for applying all 21 standards in developing or assessing particular personnel evaluation systems.

The part begins with a general procedure and then applies that procedure in an illustrative case. The case involves secondary school principals, although any personnel role could be substituted, and the general process would still apply. The final sections of this part address some of the difficulties in applying the standards and the particular issue of legal viability of personnel evaluations in education.

1.
A General Approach to
Applying the Standards

The standards were developed to enable educators to answer questions about the design, implementation, and effectiveness of a personnel evaluation system. They address such questions as the following:

"Is personnel evaluation system X well designed? (Does it look good on paper? Is the design flawed? If so, how can it be improved?)"

"Is personnel evaluation system X properly operated? (Is it being carried out in accordance with its design and accepted standards? If not, what corrective actions are indicated?)"

"Is personnel evaluation system X having the impact it should? (Does it have the intended effects? Does it have other unwanted effects? What has to be done to improve the outcomes?)"

By systematically and effectively answering these fundamental questions, institutions can assure that their evaluation systems are well conceived, being implemented correctly, and achieving the desired ends.

Steps in the Evaluation of a Personnel Evaluation System

Questions like those above could be answered by executing the following general steps:

Step 1 — Become acquainted with *The Personnel Evaluation Standards.*
Step 2 — Clarify the purposes of the evaluation system.
Step 3 — Describe the system.
Step 4 — Apply the standards.
Step 5 — Decide what to do about the results.

What is involved in implementing each of these steps is discussed below.

Step 1. Become Acquainted with the Standards

The standards are presented in non-technical language, in a common format for ease of use, and with examples to show how they can be applied. When an institution decides to use *The Personnel Evaluation Standards,* its leadership should ensure that members of evaluation committees and other interested persons, including instructors, administrators, and board members, learn and become proficient in applying the standards. These persons should be informed that the institution has adopted *The Personnel Evaluation Standards* as a basic reference by which to examine and promote quality in personnel evaluation. They should be provided copies of *The Personnel Evaluation Standards* and advised to read the entire document. Institutions should also consider offering workshops to assist their personnel to learn, discuss, and apply the standards. The aim of the orientation and training exercises should be to get institution personnel regularly to reference and use *The Personnel Evaluation Standards* as a manual for assessing and improving personnel evaluations in the institution.

Step 2. Clarify the Purposes of the Evaluation System

There are many personnel actions. No matter which one is involved, there are a number of more or less general questions. Ask (and answer) these questions:

— Whose work is to be evaluated?
— Why should the evaluations be done?
— Who will use the findings?
— What decisions will be determined or affected and/or what types of actions are evaluatees and managers expected to take in response to evaluation reports?
— Should the evaluation(s) focus on qualifications, performance, and/or effectiveness?
— What impact is the evaluation system intended to have?

Everyone should be held accountable and can benefit from sound evaluation. It is wise to make the uses and benefits explicit and seek to assure that evaluation policies and procedures are equitable across categories of personnel.

Step 3. System Description

Assemble all the documents relevant to the personnel evaluation system; e.g.:

— Policy statements and negotiated agreements
— Job descriptions, role definitions, statements of responsibilities
— Contracts or letters of employment
— Personnel policies
— Procedures manuals
— Reporting forms or rating forms

Use the documents to develop a written description of the evaluation system. Address the following questions:

— How are evaluations staffed and what are the qualifications of the evaluators?
— What are the relevant policies?
— What questions are addressed?
— What data are collected?
— How are data collected, analyzed, interpreted, and reported?
— How is the evaluation system organized, scheduled, managed, and monitored?
— What follow-up activities occur?

Next, examine the description and the supporting documents to determine whether they contain sufficient information to apply each of the 21 standards. If the information is insufficient to apply one or more standards, the evaluation system design is incomplete and more decisions need to be made. For example, certain standards require that the documents make clear the intended uses of the evaluations; the role of the evaluatee; the procedures for checking, controlling, and accessing data; the procedures for checking the validity and reliability of the data; and possible actions to be taken through personnel evaluation. If the description and assembled documents do not do that, the evaluation system description is deficient; and appropriate decisions should be reached and written down.

Step 4. Apply the Standards

Convene the judges, those persons who will examine the documentation, and have them assess the extent to which they believe each standard has been satisfied. The judges might be outside experts, experienced internal evaluators, experienced personnel specialists, members of the board, representatives of each category of evaluatee, or some mixture of users and experts.

Construct an analysis form similar to the one in Table 2 for use in summarizing judgments of the system's evaluation design. Following application of the standards, judges can use this form to record their decisions about how effectively standards are addressed by the design, or met by the evaluation operations, by placing X's next to the standards in the appropriate columns.

Provide each judge copies of *The Personnel Evaluation Standards* and the summary form, and teach judges to use these materials.

One practical approach is to have the judges apply the standards as a group. For example, divide up the standards among the judges and have each judge apply each assigned standard. Ask each judge to identify and list on a sheet of paper strengths and weaknesses of the system against the relevant requirements seen in each assigned standard. At the bottom of each sheet, ask each judge to indicate her or his judgment of whether the standard was met; partially met; not met; or, in rare cases, not applicable. Then ask the judges to report their judgments to each other and to discuss their agreements and disagreements until a consensus is reached for each standard. Finally, record the consensus judgments on the summary form. This approach is

TABLE 2
Form for Applying the Standards

	Addressed and Met	Addressed and Partially Met	Addressed and Not Met	Not Addressed
Propriety				
service orientation	___	___	___	___
formal evaluation	___	___	___	___
conflict of interest	___	___	___	___
access to personnel evaluation reports	___	___	___	___
interactions with evaluatees	___	___	___	___
Utility				
constructive orientation	___	___	___	___
defined uses	___	___	___	___
evaluator credibility	___	___	___	___
functional reporting	___	___	___	___
follow-up and impact	___	___	___	___
Feasibility				
practical procedures	___	___	___	___
political viability	___	___	___	___
fiscal viability	___	___	___	___
Accuracy				
defined role	___	___	___	___
work environment	___	___	___	___
documentation of procedures	___	___	___	___
valid measurement	___	___	___	___
reliable measurement	___	___	___	___
systematic data control	___	___	___	___
bias control	___	___	___	___
monitoring evaluation systems	___	___	___	___

especially useful when time for training and collective analysis is restricted, since each judge is asked to reach individual judgments on only a few of the standards.

When time is not so limited, each judge could be asked independently to apply all 21 standards. On a separate sheet for each standard, each judge would list strengths and weaknesses and record her or his judgment of whether the standard was met, partially met, not met, or not applicable. Each judge would then record those judgments on the summary form by placing an X next to each standard in the appropriate column. The results for all judges could then be recorded on a single form and distributed to all the judges. They could next use the summary to guide their discussions toward reaching consensus judgments for all 21 standards.

Step 5. Decide What to Do About the Results

Next, the judges should discuss the results to identify the critical issues and to develop recommendations for strengthening the evaluation system. Key issues, for example, might pertain to lack of political support for the system, inadequately trained evaluators, insufficient resources for implementation, or technical deficiencies of procedures. Recommendations to address such issues might be the development of an oversight committee representing all relevant parties to the evaluations, evaluation training for system personnel, an increased evaluation budget, or selection or development of new data collection procedures and instruments.

The judges should key their search for issues and recommendations to the results of their application of the standards and should develop a general plan for the institution to use in improving the evaluation system. As much as possible, the plan should recommend who should do what, when, how, and with what level of support.

The detailed example that follows illustrates the process.

2.
A Detailed Example:
*Using the Standards in the Design,
Implementation, and Operation of a Performance
Evaluation System for Secondary School Principals*

Description of the Case

A school district was developing a system for evaluating its school principals. In the second year of the effort, the district discovered the Joint Committee's *The Personnel Evaluation Standards: How to Assess Systems for Evaluating Educators* and decided to use them to assess their system design. If that application proved beneficial, they also planned to use *The Personnel Evaluation Standards* as a basis for assessing implementation and effects of the new system. To guide their application of *The Personnel Evaluation Standards*, the district decided to employ the process described above. An evaluation committee, comprised of district teachers and administrators, was charged with developing the new system. The following is a step-by-step account of what they did.

Orientation and Preparation

All members of the committee were provided a copy of *The Personnel Evaluation Standards* and asked to read the entire document. They then met to discuss the document and decide how to apply it to their work. At this orientation session, they divided up the 21 standards so that each of the seven members would apply three of the standards. They agreed to apply *The Personnel Evaluation Standards* to the district's teacher evaluation system, which was well established and summarized in a 5-page document. To record their individual assessments, they completed a common form for each assigned standard. It required listing strengths and weaknesses of the system against the standard, then recording whether the standard was met, partially met, not met, or not applicable. They then reported on each standard and attempted to reach a consensus judgment for each. At the end of this exercise, they agreed they were sufficiently oriented to the content of *The Personnel Evaluation Standards* to feel comfortable in applying them to the principal evaluation project.

Thus, they defined a process for making that application. Basically, they decided to adopt the process described earlier in this part. They would clarify the purposes of the principal evaluation system, describe the proposed system, use *The Personnel Evaluation Standards* to evaluate the described system, then develop their collective conclusions and recommendations. This time each member would individually apply all 21 standards before sharing and discussing her or his judgments with the other members.

Clarifying the Purpose of the Evaluation System

The Committee agreed on an agenda of questions to address. The questions and the answers they developed were as follows:

Whose performance is to be evaluated by the system? All school principals.

Why are they to be evaluated? The main reason given for the decision to evaluate was a sincere desire to help improve the quality of the principals' educational leadership. Other reasons expressed were external pressures to take visible actions to improve education, pressures from the teacher's union to evaluate somebody in addition to teachers, a belief by the superintendent that some principals were less competent or proficient than desired, and a belief by some key administrators that one or more school principals might one day become serious candidates for the superintendent's job.

Who are the interested parties? The principals; the teachers, administrators, and other educators who work with them; the superintendent; the board; the union; and the students and community served by the schools.

What actions might be taken? Initially, the school system hadn't been sure what actions it would take. District leaders thought the evaluations could be done for a while and that uses of the information could be decided later. However, early in the process of developing the principal evaluation system, the purposes were clarified. The primary purpose was to provide feedback to guide each principal to develop competence and improve performance; the secondary purpose was to provide guidance for remediating deficient performance.

To what extent should evaluations focus on the evaluatee's qualifications, performance, or effectiveness? Mainly, the principal evaluations will assess performance of assigned duties and achievement of annual administrative goals.

What are the intended impacts? Through the evaluations the district hopes to raise and make visible the standards of principal performance, assist principals to strengthen their services, and project an image in the community and the school district of professionalism and accountability.

Description of the Proposed Principal Evaluation System

After describing the purposes of the evaluation system, the Evaluation Committee described the system thus far designed to evaluate the principals.

In compliance with the process adopted for evaluating the design, the Committee first compiled all relevant documents. These included the written charge from the superintendent, the minutes of their meetings, the collective bargaining agreement, the board policy on personnel evaluation, and the latest draft of the design. Other materials included the performance evaluation procedures previously adopted for teachers, and procedures agreed upon but not yet implemented for auxiliary service personnel.

Using the above materials, the Committee next determined and addressed an agenda of questions to describe the current version of the principal evaluation design. The questions and the Committee's responses were as follows:

Who is in charge of designing the principal evaluation system, what is their responsibility and authority, and what are their qualifications? The Evaluation Committee had been convened by the superintendent and given a broad charge to design procedures for evaluating secondary school principals. The committee members represented a cross section of constituencies within the district and included principals, classroom teachers, curriculum specialists, an assistant superintendent, and a representative from the personnel department. No member had been specially trained in personnel evaluation.

What are the relevant policies?   The board adopted a policy statement that said the appraisal process was intended to:

— encourage continual professional growth
— identify both strengths and weaknesses
— encourage participation by those evaluated
— recognize excellence
— provide remedies for deficient performances that failed to contribute to a productive professional and educational environment

The remedies included informal counseling, professional development course work, transfers to more suitable duties, and, as a last resort, termination.

What are the major evaluation questions?   The major evaluation question was, "To what extent is each principal fulfilling her or his assigned responsibilities and achieving stated goals in the areas of leadership, staff development, administration, public relations, and professional growth?" Questions about credentials and prior experience were not considered relevant, since those areas had been assessed at the time the principals were hired or promoted to the principalship. Moreover, principals were not to be evaluated based upon the standardized test results of students in their schools.

What data are needed to answer the evaluation questions?   Individual objectives were to be set, and the relevant data would be decided upon when that was done.

How shall the data be collected, analyzed, interpreted, and reported, and what follow-up activities will occur?   Each principal was to be evaluated by an assistant superintendent, who would be given a set of guidelines to follow and an orientation session led by the committee representative from Personnel. The guidelines specified that the following activities were to occur:

1. Each of the three assistant superintendents was to arrange for a goal-setting meeting with each assigned principal. The pur-

poses of the evaluation were to be explained to the principals, goals for the year discussed, and a follow-up meeting scheduled.

2. Goals for the year were to be set at the second meeting and an observation schedule worked out.

3. The observation schedule was to require a minimum of three observations related to each goal (several goals could be assessed during each observation). The assistant superintendent and principal were to agree on a visitation schedule that would provide ample opportunity to observe relevant performances, but they were not to be scheduled so tightly that the principal knew to the day when each visit would occur.

4. Conferences were to be scheduled after each visit; there would be discussions of what the assistant superintendent observed and any significant weaknesses pointed out immediately.

5. The assistant superintendent would write a summary report, providing the principal with a copy at least two weeks before an "annual review" conference to be held in May.

6. A plan for improvement would then be submitted by the principal before the end of the school year.

7. The improvement plan, if approved by the assistant superintendent, would be the basis of professional development work during the summer and the basis of the goal-setting conference in the fall.

How is the evaluation to be managed, scheduled, and monitored? The Assistant Superintendent for Administration would manage the system with technical support from the Personnel Department. The plan followed the same general timeframe and procedures as the performance evaluations performed for teachers and other education professionals within the principal's building. (The principals would regularly attend an orientation and updating session each fall relevant to their evaluating responsibilities.) The Evaluation Committee was assigned, annually, to monitor, evaluate, and make recommendations for improving the system.

Each principal was to prepare for the initial goal-setting conference by reviewing his or her position description. (There were different descriptions for elementary, middle, and secondary school principals.) Further, each principal was to come prepared with goals for five major areas of responsibilities:

Curricular leadership
Staff morale/staff development

School administration
Public relations
Professional growth

The Committee, in presenting the plan to the board, had argued that the plan was appropriate for the principals, who should be able to set worthy goals for the year. The principals and assistant superintendents were in the best position to determine whether each goal had been achieved; the summative report should contain any data needed to support their perceptions.

The annual summary report would contain the assistant superintendents' recommendations regarding pay increases, remediation, potential for promotion, and the like.

The board had become persuaded that the plan should be implemented on a trial basis to see if it helped and to identify any serious, unanticipated flaws.

Applying the Standards:
Case Specific Comments

After updating the description of the principal evaluation system, the Committee turned to the task of evaluating the evaluation plan against the 21 Joint Committee standards.

They carried on the discussion in a standard by standard sequence, asking one member to record the strengths and weaknesses and the Committee's judgments about the extent that each standard was met. Subsequently, they reviewed their judgments for all of the standards and summarized their main conclusions, which were as follows:

Propriety Standards

The Committee decided that, overall, the plan was strong in relation to the propriety standards but that certain deficiencies were evident and needed to be addressed.

They noted that the system was weak in its **Service Orientation**. While it was constructed to help principals improve their performance, it did not provide explicitly for dismissing or reassigning principals who persisted in performing substandard work. Accordingly, the Committee decided to work with the superintendent to define due process steps for dismissing a principal who was found to be deficient in performance and who subsequently did not respond effectively to remediation steps.

The Committee thought their work in preparing to apply *The Personnel Evaluation Standards* had helped them to document the guidelines for applying the evaluation system and decided they were making satisfactory progress toward meeting the requirements of the **Formal Guidelines** standard. They agreed that, after further review and refinement of the system, a formal set of guidelines for the system should be presented by the superintendent to the board for formal adoption.

They identified a possible **Conflict of Interest** problem in that some of the principals would likely become candidates for promotion to posts held or sought by the assistant superintendents who were slated to evaluate the principals. If an assistant superintendent was worried about actual or potential competition with a principal, it could be difficult for her or him to remain unbiased. They saw the design as flawed in that respect and decided to modify it or build in safeguards. Ideas to be pursued at a later time would include formalizing an appeal process or establishing routine procedures whereby principals could submit material in rebuttal. They also thought that in obvious conflicts of interest, other equally or more credible evaluators should be found.

Turning to the **Access to Personnel Evaluation Reports**, the Committee noted the evaluation plan failed to address this standard and decided they must write a section to clarify who had access to the principal evaluation reports. They decided to check the district's standard policies on access to personnel information and to reference those in clarifying the access provisions in the principal evaluation plan.

Finally, in relation to the Propriety Standards, the Committee agreed it would be important to monitor closely the **Interactions with Evaluatees** standard during implementation. The designers' intentions in that regard should be spelled out in the **Evaluation Guidelines** and the system monitored to assure that the evaluation promoted and supported, rather than detracted, from positive relations between the principals, central office administrators, and the Personnel Department.

Utility Standards

The Committee judged the design to be strong with respect to the Utility Standards, but they identified problems to be addressed in revising the design or in evaluating the first round of implementation.

The **orientation** of the plan was deemed **constructive**, as reflected in the desire to use the evaluations to help the principals improve their performance and since performance weaknesses were to be documented far enough in advance of the annual summary report to allow early corrections. Further corrections could become the basis of goal setting during the next annual cycle.

There were **Defined Uses** of the evaluations. The primary **use** of the system seemed to be as a coaching or management-by-objectives system. Also, based on their response, noted above, to the Service Orientation standard, the Committee intended to revise the system to identify deficient performance, provide for remediation, and, when these steps did not work, to provide a basis for dismissals. It was not clear exactly how the evaluations would be used equitably in dismissal. (More will be said about this under the discussion of the Accuracy Standards.)

An adequate measure of **Evaluator Credibility** was likely because the principals had been heavily involved in the process and had numerous opportunities to raise objections if they were uneasy about the ability of the assistant superintendents to perform the evaluations. Also, the Evaluation Committee represented a cross section of district personnel and was duly authorized to design the system. In addition, the central administration backed the development and was committed to manage implementation with support from the Personnel Department. However, the system's potential to meet this standard rests largely on the process used in developing the system. The Evaluation Committee apparently believed that the principals would find the assistant superintendents to be credible evaluators. The principals were represented on the committee and did not oppose the proposal to the board. Nevertheless, there were pitfalls concerning credibility of the assistant superintendents that needed to be watched carefully during implementation.

There was **Functional Reporting** because of the timely conferences.

The use of reports to update goals and plan for the next year would help bring about positive **Impacts**. However, as yet, the process for removing incompetent principals had not been defined.

Feasibility Standards

The design with respect to the feasibility standards was generally sound but manifested some weaknesses.

There were both strengths and weaknesses regarding the **Practical Procedures** standard. The procedures were simple and easy to understand and the observations could be scheduled so that they would not be disruptive. However, there was a potential problem with **Practical Procedures** because of scheduling problems. The principals were going to be doing evaluations of teachers and auxiliary personnel; since these would occur on approximately the same time cycle as the evaluations of the principals, scheduling could become a nightmare. The principal's evaluation could interfere with the evaluations the principal was performing or, worse, lead to hastily performed evaluations.

The **Political Viability** standard was quite well addressed. There was input from a variety of persons in the district, including the evaluatees, in the development of the evaluation system. Also, the system was being reviewed and assessed against professional standards, and the process was not being rushed. Moreover, the evaluation system is clearly subject to revision, when deficiencies became apparent. However, the board had not made a clear commitment to support the system, and the Superintendent would need to increase the board's understanding of the system, obtain their suggestions, and earn their support of it.

The procedures were not costly and incorporated follow-up through repeated evaluation cycles. Since few resources would be expended, the costs of any personnel decisions and recommendations would be low. Nevertheless, **Fiscal Viability** should be monitored during the operation of the performance evaluation system. The current lack of concern about costs may prove to be optimistic.

Accuracy Standards

Accuracy standards were somewhat problematic in this design. If the principals and assistant superintendents were unusually skilled in measurement of complex performances, the system might work well; however, it would not be good practice to take for granted that all the principals and assistant superintendents would be uniformly and highly competent in performance measurement. (One might expect, given the current state of the art, that improvement in ability to assess performance accurately would be an important goal for some of the principals.) Even if exceptional ability in this area is assumed, careful monitoring would be prudent.

The design was based upon a reasonably well **Defined Role** for the principals in that the system specified the key areas of their performance to be evaluated. Also, the system provided that each year's evaluation feedback would be used to update performance goals. Nevertheless, the role of the principal should be specified in more detail. While it is possible that each principal would have an understanding of what must be done to perform well in the five designated areas, it is quite unlikely that all principals have the same understanding. It is also extremely unlikely that each assistant superintendent would have the same understanding as the principal being evaluated.

It might be safe to assume (pending data from implementation) that any constraints from the **Work Environment** would be considered when the principals and assistant superintendents negotiated the goals. However, there were insufficient provisions for determining and taking into account the constraints of the Work Environment.

The progress toward **Documentation of Procedures** is good but not sufficient. The design was well **described**, but it would be wise to ascertain that it is adequately understood by all parties. (This checking should be done as part of the evaluation of the implementation. It should also be determined that actual procedures follow the design.) There was some uncertainty about just how the summary reports were intended to be used in making personnel decisions regarding dismissal. The fact that this was not clear was a serious flaw in the design.

There were serious questions about whether or not the planned evaluation procedures would yield **Valid and Reliable Measurement**. The only data source and data collection technique specified in the design would come from the assistant superintendents' observation visits. It is possible that the assistant superintendents would examine a variety of documents, examine data collected in the school, interview key personnel, and systematically observe the principal in action in a variety of roles; however, this would be too much to hope for and should not be left to chance. The present data collection plan rested too heavily on one supervisor's observations; it should be supplemented with plans to collect data on work environment, on performance of all job dimensions, and on achievement of annual goals. In order to enhance and check reliability, several different data collection procedures should be employed.

Systematic Data Control might not be a problem with the small amounts of data involved, but the design would be strengthened if some mention were made of where the reports would be stored and where raw observation data or notes would be kept and for how long. Systematic data control would also strengthen the system with respect to the Monitoring Evaluation Systems standard, as it would assure that it would be possible to examine the notes and observations and do an independent assessment of the extent to which the conclusions and recommendations were based upon the observations or upon other unknown factors.

Given the potential conflict of interest problem already mentioned, getting **Unbiased Interpretation** would be a concern. It was a significant soft spot in the design and should be watched carefully during the implementation period and thereafter. Also, accurate Interpretation of observations by the assistant superintendents was another potential problem area. One would hope that the principal and the superintendent would reach agreement about the meaning of the observations, either during the negotiation of the goals or during post-observation conferences. For example, the observation that only one teacher sought a principal's advice during three observation periods might be a plus for one principal (who needs to avoid meddling in classroom affairs) and a minus for another (who needs to improve communications with the teaching staff). Another difficulty with interpretation occurs to the extent that the appraisals would be used in making other personnel decisions. The criteria for judging a principal's performance *as principal* should probably differ from those used to judge the suitability for promotion to another function, as anyone knows who has seen an excellent principal become a marginal superintendent.

The **Monitoring Evaluation Systems** standard was at least partially satisfied in that the system was reviewed by a constituent committee and also by the board. Depending upon the inclinations and inquisitiveness of the board, the design could receive a thorough or cursory review.

Recommendations Based
Upon the Analysis

A good start was made in designing the performance evalua-tion system, but there were some problem areas. The system was likely to be both **Useful** and **Feasible**. There was a potential **Propriety** problem in the possible conflict of interest because each assistant superintendent was assigned to evaluate persons with whom he or she might be in competition for a job in the future, because their assessments were not combined with other, more objective data. Moreover, the **Accuracy** of the information was also problematic. Specific recommendations for design changes are listed in Table 3.

TABLE 3
Recommendations for Design Changes

Propriety Standards

Service Orientation	Clarify the process for citing and addressing deficiencies and, when necessary, dismissing an ineffective principal.
Formal evaluation guidelines	Be sure to describe guidelines fully, in an accessible document. Additional guidelines should be added as problems are encountered.
Conflict of interest	Potential problem. Build in safeguards to deal with competition for advancement between evaluator and evaluatee. Make sure that the assistant superintendent is not the sole agent in the evaluation, provide for receiving and appending reactions by the evaluatee, and provide an appeal process.
Access to personnel evaluation reports	Clarify by a specific policy statement.
Interactions with evaluatees	OK in design but monitor implementation and address any pervasive or recurrent problems.

Utility Standards

Constructive orientation	OK in design but it should be monitored; as the process for remediation and possible dismissal is clarified, there will likely be increased tension between the constructive orientation and service orientation standards.
Defined uses	Specify more clearly how the appraisal will be used for dismissal or other personnel decisions.

Evaluator credibility	A good start has been made but much work remains. Assistant superintendents will need appropriate training and the Evaluation Committee will need to carry out their monitoring role effectively. Also, the superintendent and board must demonstrate a strong commitment to make the system work.
Functional reporting	OK. Conferences are timely and relevant.
Follow-up and impact	OK in design but it should be monitored; assessing impacts on the performance of principals should be a key responsibility of the Evaluation Committee as they evaluate implementation and seek ways to improve the system.

Feasibility Standards

Practical procedures	OK, but consider possible scheduling problems due to the principals' responsibilities for evaluating teachers and auxiliary personnel.
Political viability	So far very good, but it will be important for the superintendent to bring the board more directly into the process of adopting and using the system.
Fiscal viability	OK, but monitor costs during the first year both to seek efficiencies and to identify any parts of the system that are underfunded.

Accuracy Standards

Defined role	A good start has been made. The five areas of responsibility should be clarified immediately or during the first few years the system is used. Also, the specifics of each principal's job should be clarified annually. Specify, at the outset of the evaluation, that the evaluator and principal each list the standards that they believe are appropriate for judging performance. Emphasize that the evaluation should consider both the general and specific characteristics of the job and the priorities for the year.
Work environment	Probably OK, but assistant superintendents should be encouraged to make specific reference to relevant constraints in their reports.
Valid measurement	Be sure that evaluators are adequately trained in relevant measurement techniques. Direct and assist assistant superintendents to use a variety of data sources in their evaluations. The specific data sources should be dictated by the specific jobs, situations, and goals.

TABLE 3 (Cont.)

Reliable measurement	Keep findings from different sources separate until they can be checked for consistency. Use instances of inconsistency in redesigning the data collection procedures and in further training of the assistant superintendents.
Systematic data control	Clarify in the guidelines where the evaluation records are to be kept, how they will be checked for accuracy, and who will protect the integrity of the information.
Bias control	Build in additional safeguards (e.g., consider having the work of the evaluators reviewed by the superintendent and/or a committee from the board).
Monitoring evaluation systems	Assigning the Evaluation Committee to study implementation of the system was an excellent move. Make sure their charge is clear, that they have sufficient time and resources to do the job, and that the superintendent and board are predisposed to address the Committee's findings and recommendations. Project an annual report that assesses compliance with these 21 standards.

If the committee accepted the ongoing responsibility for evaluating the system, they would be the appropriate body to consider the recommendations for improving the design and considering and carrying out recommendations such as those in Table 4.

TABLE 4
Recommendations for Evaluating the Implementation and the Effectiveness of the System

Propriety Standards

Service orientation	Randomly sample goals stated and achieved, and have these goals critiqued for the extent to which meeting them would serve students and community. The critiques could be obtained from the board or a citizens review panel.
Formal evaluation guidelines	Have some of the principals review the written guidelines periodically to assess the extent to which the evaluator followed them.
Conflict of interest	Periodically survey evaluators and evaluatees to determine whether they perceive actual or potential conflict of interest problems.

Access to personnel evaluation reports	Establish a records control system that makes it possible to control access to evaluation records. Assign responsibility for maintaining the record controls.
Interactions with evaluators	Have principals evaluate the interactions they have with evaluators, colleagues, or administrators.

Utility Standards

Constructive orientation	Have principals evaluate the conferences and the summary reports regarding the perceived constructive orientation of the system in use.
Defined uses	Monitor to assure that the actual uses do not grow to include uses that were not intended and/or to assure that new uses are incorporated fully into the system.
Evaluator credibility	Monitor to assure that the assistant superintendents' evaluations are, in fact, generally credible.
Functional reporting	Monitor to assure that the system of conferences deals adequately with weaknesses and/or changing conditions.
Follow-up and impact	Have all evaluatees and evaluators periodically provide perceptions of their overall confidence in the system. Monitor compliance with the system to assure that it is not just perfunctory.

Feasibility Standards

Practical procedures	Monitor the ease of use of the system, looking especially at possible scheduling problems and peak work load problems.
Political viability	Survey all evaluatees and evaluators to determine whether they believe their interests and values are adequately represented.
Fiscal viability	Have some of the evaluators and evaluatees maintain records of the time required to do the evaluation process properly. Consider the need for and cost of additional training, clerical support, and the like.

Accuracy Standards

Defined role	Review and summarize the job descriptions and annual goals. Assess the degree to which the jobs and goals are both clear and oriented to the principal's pervasive responsibility to promote excellence and improvement in the school. Reflect the results of this assessment in the Committee's annual monitoring report.

TABLE 4 (Cont.)

Work environment	Have assistant superintendents meet to review work environment constraints and to identify removable obstacles, facilitating conditions, and apparent constraints being used as excuses.
Documentation of procedures	Have one or two of the principals, on a rotating basis, review the descriptions and the actual procedures to see if they match.
Valid measurement	An important approach to validity for the purposes of this system is content validity. Summarize all of the information sources used by the assistant superintendents to measure goal attainment. Have a panel comprised of a cross section of local educators review the sources to make judgments of adequacy or suggestions for additional or more appropriate sources.
Reliable measurement	Assess reliability in terms of repeated measures across observations. The review should also consider consistency across evaluators. Establishing a proper range of information sources would make it possible to assess interobserver correspondence by having teachers and/or auxiliary personnel observe some of the performances observed by the assistant superintendents.
Systematic data control	Establish policies regarding storage of the records of observations; assign responsibility for implementing the policy to an administrative assistant from the superintendent's office, who will maintain and control access to the records.
Bias control	Monitor the summary reports written by the assistant superintendents to assure that they have made the criteria that were used explicitly clear. The superintendent should also review the reports to assure that the interpretations are consistent with the values expressed during the goal-setting phase (and that those values are consistent with the district's philosophy).
Monitoring evaluation systems	The committee should develop a coherent evaluation plan to implement the above recommendations and answer other evaluation questions the committee might have.

General Aspects of the Case

Use of *The Personnel Evaluation Standards* revealed a number of potential pitfalls and needed changes. The first and foremost recommendation to be considered by the district was to underscore the importance of charging the Evaluation Committee to evaluate the adequacy-in-operation of the system and its effectiveness. Should the district decide not to do that, it is unlikely that the other recommendations would be implemented effectively. In that event, the recommendations are superfluous. It is quite likely that the performance evaluation system would also soon become superfluous.

The committee that designed the system probably would have felt a sense of accomplishment and closure once the system was accepted by the board. But designs and plans are only the beginning. The work begins in earnest during the first couple of years while the performance evaluation is still in a "shake-down" or formative stage.

There are some quite predictable occurrences in the development of a new evaluation system. The developers of the system should try to anticipate such occurrences, be ready to address them, identify such occurrences as early as possible, and then address them in a constructive manner. Some of the things that the Committee might watch out for during the first year are:

1. At least one principal/assistant superintendent pair would agree readily on goals but have difficulty agreeing upon criteria and measures. As a result, the conferences would deteriorate into mutual defensiveness, probably cloaked in civility.

2. At least one principal/assistant superintendent pair would perform the process in an exemplary manner and be thoroughly satisfied. Another would perform the process well but be somewhat suspicious of each other's "real" feelings about the reasons why some of the goals were not achieved.

3. The superintendent would believe that the goals set by most of the principals were "safe," rather than "challenging."

4. At least 33% of the conference reports would be late, many of the May conferences would be late, the end-of-year improvement plans would be cursory, and the assistant superintendents would not have time to review them carefully and request improvements.

5. Some principals would start the second year of the system with greater confidence and enthusiasm. Others would be ready

to go through the motions if the assistant superintendent pushed them, but would feel they were participating in the demise of another misadventure in performance evaluation.

The first year would be characterized by a hopeful willingness to try the system, but the second year is more likely to be critical. During the second year the novelty has worn off, and those who like developing new systems better than the work of follow-through would probably turn their attention to other tasks. The second year would begin the test of the real commitment to making the system work.

If the design committee does not work hard to make the system work, and if the assistant superintendents, principals, and other participants do not cooperate, the lack of commitment will be apparent and the system will decay. More (rather than fewer) of the pairs will not function well, although the exemplary pairs might still continue to operate effectively. The goals would become more perfunctory, rather than more challenging. More scheduling problems would occur and more (rather than fewer) conference reports would be late. The improvement plans would become less rather than more satisfactory. Instead of becoming a tool for development, the system would evolve into a bureaucratic chore. The fate of best laid plans that lack the commitment of follow-up is well known. Performance evaluation systems are not immune from that fate.

We have been able to think of no better alternative to having an ongoing committee charged with the responsibility for assuring that the performance evaluation system "grows" into a properly functioning system. A strong superintendent can convene the committee; but a representative body needs to assume leadership and responsibility for the performance evaluation system, lest it fall into decay and become a source of acrimonious discussions between evaluatees (as a group) and evaluators (as a group). In addition, it is crucial that the superintendent keep the board both informed and convinced that they should support the evaluation system and hold the staff accountable for making it work.

The closest viable alternative to responsibility by a representative body is to attempt to integrate the performance evaluation system firmly into the fabric of the organization. A case could be made for making performance evaluation itself a major responsibility of every educational leader. For example, a secondary school principal might very well allocate 25 percent or more of his or her working time to duties associated with performance evaluation. If a strong *Constructive Orientation* and a strong *Service Orientation* were hallmarks of the system, it could be a major tool for fulfilling the principal's role as an educator. Helping the teaching and auxiliary staff develop themselves to provide better service to students and community is a central, not a tangential, function of the principal. It is only through the work of the teachers and auxiliary staff that the educational mission can be fulfilled.

The "traditional" view of performance evaluation would not, of course, support such a time investment. The view of performance evaluation as just another task piled upon other, more important tasks does not condone such an investment. Performance evaluation, done as an add-on task by an overworked principal—who does not know how to do it or why it is required or what its real value is—has not been worth 20 percent of a principal's time. On the other hand, the traditional view and traditional practice of performance evaluation are hardly models to emulate.

The standards have been developed to guide educators to install and implement sound evaluation systems. The secondary school principal case illustrates a good use of the standards to:

1. Design a performance evaluation system that fits the local situation.

2. Focus on one or two major purposes (at least at first), rather than trying to design a system that would serve every conceivable purpose.

3. Design the system with the full participation of those most closely involved, calling upon the best they have to offer.

4. Use *The Personnel Evaluation Standards* to evaluate the design. It would be better to evaluate the first draft, rather than the one approved by the board.

5. Use *The Personnel Evaluation Standards* to help define the responsibilities of those who are to be in charge of getting the system installed, debugged, and functioning effectively.

6. Keep improving the system as those involved in it gain greater expertise, as new techniques are discovered, as new problems are encountered, and as successes lead to new challenges.

Difficulties in Applying the Standards

The procedures that were used in this Application Section do not guarantee that all problems will be anticipated and solved by using *The Personnel Evaluation Standards* to evaluate or design a personnel evaluation system. Unfortunately, there are many unknowns in the practice of personnel evaluation; and, while *The Personnel Evaluation Standards* represent the best thinking of many knowledgeable, experienced people about sound general principles for personnel evaluation, there remain issues that may have to be resolved when the standards are applied. Not all of the questions that may surface when applying the standards can be predicted, but we can begin to develop a list. Some things to consider:

1. There may be a lack of common understanding or agreement about the components of good performance and how to measure them. Allow time to engage in reflective discussion with interested persons and to work through a process of developing common understandings.

2. There are some inclined to evaluate personal characteristics rather than qualifications, performance, or effectiveness. Be certain to aim the standards at evaluations of qualifications, performance, or effectiveness.

3. There may be ambiguity about who is to receive personal evaluation reports, and how they are to use them. Be sure these aspects of the system are clearly understood and that safeguards are used whenever necessary to avoid misuse of reports.

4. There may be times, such as during reductions in force, when the ground rules for the personnel evaluation system change. *The Personnel Evaluation Standards* should be reapplied whenever the system changes.

5. There may be a predisposition to direct personnel evaluation only at achievement of performance goals, overlooking unintended or unexpected achievements. *The Personnel Evaluation Standards* remind us to broaden our scope beyond the expected or intended.

6. There may be a feeling of hopelessness, a stifling effect, when the standards are applied and many deficiencies or inadequate resources prevent the operation of an ideal personnel evaluation system. Educators should keep in mind that few things in life are ideal and that the intended use of the *The Personnel*

Evaluation Standards is to guide the practice of personnel evaluation in the best *possible* way. Development of a high quality evaluation system is a project that can be done over an extended period of time.

7. There will be times when it is difficult to decide whether a standard has been met. Professional judgments are required in applying the standards. A committee of stakeholders and qualified consultants may enhance the soundness and defensibility of those judgments.

This list will probably grow and be revised as we gain experience in using the standards. As we learn more about how to apply them and about the unresolved issues that even now can be foreseen, we plan to share that knowledge in future editions of *The Personnel Evaluation Standards*.

Legal Viability

We conclude this part by commenting on the particular issue of legal viability of personnel evaluations.

Experience has shown that personnel evaluations often lead to legal proceedings; indeed, there has been, and probably will continue to be, an overall increase in the amount of legal activity concerning educational employee evaluations. Despite the extent of legal issues inherent in the evaluation of educational personnel, this book contains no standard on legal viability. Such a standard would be necessarily general and, hence, of limited utility for those developing and implementing an evaluation system.

The vast body of legal mandates contained in the constitution and laws of the United States, the constitution and statutes of each state, local laws, case law, the provisions and interpretations of negotiated contracts, and organizational policies and regulations create a complex set of standards within which the 21 standards in this book must be applied. Of necessity, the evaluation system should meet the requirements of all federal, state, and local laws, as well as those of case law, contractual agreements, and local board policies and regulations or university statutes or bylaws. However, laws, statutes, rules, and legal precedents pertaining to personnel evaluation vary from locale to locale.

There are, however, some common threads running through many of these legal requirements. All of the applicable legal standards will, at a minimum, include basic due process requirements. Many of the requirements of basic due process will be met if the standards set forth in this book are followed. In this respect, these personnel evaluation standards serve as a good set of guidelines not only for implementing good evaluation practices but also for avoiding many types of legal difficulties. For example, due process requires that, when a public employer is going to dismiss a teacher under contract or terminate a tenured teacher, it must provide sufficient advanced notice of the criteria for its decision making and of the action it proposes to take against a teacher. Further, due process requires an opportunity for an employee to know the standards against which he or she will be judged. Several of these personnel evaluation standards should, if they are carefully followed, help employers begin to meet the requirements of due process of law and should afford educational employees the types of protections that due process guarantees them.

The standard on *functional reporting* and its requirement for clear and timely reports to employees should be of assistance in guiding users toward the goal of meeting the notice requirements of due process. Similarly, the articulation of clearly *defined roles* for education personnel enhances the defensibility under due process requirements of a determination that an employee failed to meet her or his responsibilities. Another basic element of due process is the requirement that adequate procedures be utilized in making significant decisions about personnel to ensure fairness in decision making. The standard on practical procedures and the Accuracy Standards, particularly those encouraging the use of sufficient samples of performance and the use of *valid measurement* and *reliable measurement*, should be of help in meeting some of the procedural requirements of due process.

These standards cannot, of course, help users avoid all legal pitfalls, even those arising from due process requirements. One typical problem is the use of evaluative information to make significant judgments about a person's work when the information arises from a context outside the person's usual scope of work responsibility. Court cases often arise over efforts to dismiss education personnel because they criticized the superintendent of schools or university president or because they engaged in some behavior outside of work that the community considered socially unacceptable. An employer might follow all of the standards set forth in this book to gather, confirm, and assess such information about an employee and still make a judgment that could lead to serious legal difficulty. Such situations are, however, often the types of cases in which courts might well determine that the employer's decision should be affirmed if the employer is able to articulate a clear, rational, and coherent link between the stated missions and purposes of the educational institution and the previously unstated criterion to which the employee is now being held. For example, few teacher evaluation systems, no matter how carefully they were implemented under these standards, would articulate a requirement that elementary and secondary teachers refrain from publicly advocating racist policies and practices, or encouraging youngsters to use illegal drugs. Yet, we believe no court would require the continued employment of a teacher who engages in such activity since it would be so inimical to the basic goals of a school. Great care must be taken by educational employers in assessing evaluative information gathered outside the ordinary system of evaluation developed and implemented under these standards to ensure that the criteria they use for their decisions are clearly legitimate, given the well-articulated missions of their educational enterprise and the role definitions of the employees. To some extent, certain of these standards, such as those requiring a *defined role* for evaluatees and *valid measures* of conduct, should be of some value in doing this. To a larger extent, however, clear-headed professional judgment will be an employer's best guide.

Aside from due process requirements present in any state, some particular state law requirements should also be easier to meet for those employers who adhere to the standards. For example, attention to the standard on *access to personnel evaluation reports* should be of assistance in aiding compliance with state laws, local policies, or contractual provisions governing the confidentiality of personnel records.

Even following the standard on *human interaction* carefully and thoughtfully might be of use in avoiding legal difficulty by diminishing the sorts of interpersonnel frictions that often lead to unnecessary lawsuits resulting from breakdowns in smooth professional communications.

It is of paramount importance that the development of a personnel evaluation system include consultation with an attorney who is very familiar with the laws governing the employment and evaluation of educational personnel in the particular setting. There is a good deal that such an expert can do to minimize the potential for future legal complications by ensuring that the policies and procedures included in the personnel evaluation system meet requisite legal requirements. Use of an attorney or legal expert is a necessary but not sufficient condition; care must be taken to ensure that a personnel evaluation system is designed for the context in which it is to be used. Personnel evaluation systems must be both legally sound and educationally sound.

Anyone engaged in performing educational personnel evaluations must know that, sooner or later, an evaluation will be challenged in some legal proceeding, be it as relatively uncomplicated as a grievance under a collective bargaining agreement or as complex and expensive as litigation through the federal courts. It is our hope that, while compliance with these standards will not prevent legal challenges, it should, in conjunction with competent legal advice, help to minimize legal complications while at the same time promoting sound professional practice. Sound professional practice rests upon a foundation of concern for the goal of any educational enterprise; the education of students. These standards are intended to foster fair, but firm-minded evaluations to foster the achievement of that goal.

APPENDICES

A: Development of the Standards

B: Citing the Standards

C: The Support Groups

APPENDIX A

Development Of The Standards

Need for the Standards

Virtually all educational institutions in the United States evaluate the qualifications and work of at least some of their personnel—specifically, at the points of certification, selection, assignment, promotion, award of tenure, and allocation of special recognition or monetary awards. Some institutions also use evaluation to provide feedback for improving the performance of educational personnel. Parents and students use formal or informal evaluations to identify and avoid poor instructors. In sum, personnel evaluations are pervasive in educational institutions as one part of a total system designed to select, support, and assure excellent service by educators (or improve or discharge those who deliver poor service).

However, there is widespread dissatisfaction with the quality of personnel evaluation in education. Community groups, policy boards, and educators often decry the near absence of personnel evaluation in their institutions or the superficiality in the systems that do exist.

Scriven (1983) agreed that such claims are often valid. He placed much of the blame for avoidance or shallowness of personnel evaluation on a faulty view of evaluation, which, in the name of objectivity, passively leaves evaluation of performance to independent evaluators, which, he says, are often ineffective. A fundamental tenet of professionalism, says Scriven, is that true professionals must evaluate their own work and actively and openly seek to have others evaluate it.

From a somewhat different perspective, Soar, Medley, and Coker (1983, p. 246) state that teachers' resistance to evaluation is reasonable, since they consider that evaluations now in use are "subjective, unreliable, open to bias, closed to public scrutiny, and based on irrelevancies." This position is consistent with an extensive research study of teacher evaluation released by the

Rand Corporation. After an exhaustive analysis of research in operating teacher evaluation systems, Darling-Hammond et al. (1983) concluded that most existing systems are illogical, simplistic, unfair, counterproductive, or simply unproductive.

Thus, many concerned and informed groups agree that there is a need both to increase the amount and improve the quality of personnel evaluation in education.

The publication of several national reports pointing out problems and shortcomings in education has brought into even sharper focus the crucial need to evaluate and provide direction for improving the performance of educational personnel (Boyer, 1983; Carnegie Task Force on Teaching as a Profession, 1986; *Educating Americans for the 21st Century*, 1982; Goodlad, 1983; *Making the Grade*—Peterson, 1983; *A Nation at Risk*—National Commission on Excellence in Education, 1983). These reports "all acknowledge that one of the most pressing problems to be faced is attracting and retaining excellent teachers for our nation's schools" (NEA, 1983). This recognition clearly attests to the pressing need for effective and sound personnel evaluation procedures.

Extensive media coverage and political rhetoric—frequently partisan and self-interested—and debate resulting from these reports have generated a number of proposals and programs aimed at increasing and improving evaluations of educational personnel, especially teachers (Carnegie Task Force, 1986; Duke & Stiggins, 1986). Efforts in personnel evaluation have been identified with such labels as career ladders, professional and basic skills tests, merit pay, peer evaluation, master teachers, clinical supervision, assessment centers, and national certification.

Some of these responses oversimplify the problems involved in assessing educators' performance. However, they have captured public attention, and educators are faced with both a problem and an opportunity. They could become unwitting accomplices in efforts that impair education if they accept simplistic solutions. However, they could help move the profession forward if, as one avenue of action, they convince the public that improved educator performance requires sound programs for evaluating education personnel.

State education departments, school districts, and policy analysts are addressing the public concern for improving education by moving aggressively to devise better systems for evaluating personnel. Several states have developed new evaluation systems on which to base decisions about certification, incentive pay, and career advancement. Examples at the state level include the Career Ladder Program in Tennessee (Furtwengler, McLarty, & Malo, 1985), the evaluation of prospective teachers in Connecticut and Michigan, the systematic observation and rating of first year teachers in Florida, and the testing of teachers in Alabama, Arkansas, and Texas. A number of school districts are implementing the clinical supervision approaches advocated by Madeline Hunter (*Teaching Is Decision Making*, 1979), Richard Manatt et al. (*Evaluating Teacher Performance with Improved Rating Scales*, 1976), and others; and reports by the Educational Research Service, Inc. (1976, 1983) reflect a number of interesting developments in education personnel evaluation.

One in-depth investigation of teacher evaluation systems was conducted by the Rand Corporation, who conducted case studies of four school districts selected to represent diverse teacher evaluation processes and organizational environments. These included the peer evaluation system in Toledo, Ohio; the shared governance approach in Salt Lake City; the clinical supervision approach as in effect in Lake Washington, Washington; and the management and evaluation by objectives approach as practiced in Greenwich, Connecticut. While these districts went about their evaluation tasks in different ways, they had in common four practices that the study team viewed as responsible for the superiority of these evaluation programs (Wise, Darling-Hammond, McLaughlin, & Bernstein, 1984). These "superiority factors" were "organizational commitment, evaluator competence, teacher-administrator collaboration, and strategic compatibility."

In addition to developments in teacher evaluation, work is being done to improve evaluation of administrators. Of particular relevance are the assessment centers for selecting school principals, sponsored by the National Association of Secondary School Principals (Cascio & Silbey, 1979; Hersey, 1987; Moses & Ritchie, 1976; Schmitt, Noe, Merritt, Fitzgerald, & Jorgensen, n.d.; Task Force on Assessment Center Standards, 1979; Thornton & Byham, 1982; Wexley & Latham, 1982). Evaluation of the performance of school district superintendents was the topic of a monograph issued by the Illinois Association of School Boards (Booth & Glaub, 1978).

The above-mentioned field-based efforts are responsive to the problems of educational personnel evaluation, and apparently many are proceeding under careful and informed direction, with political and monetary support. In addition to addressing local problems unique to particular communities, these programs have the potential to provide operational models that can be adopted or adapted by other school districts and state education departments. But if either of these ends is to be realized, new and innovative systems need to be assessed against and made to satisfy widely accepted principles of sound personnel evaluation. Only then can both public and educational institutions be confident that their efforts to improve the quality and effectiveness of personnel evaluation are proceeding appropriately and effectively. The Rand study's identification of success factors is an important step in the right direction, but further investigation and wider involvement are needed.

A major problem is that the professions of education and evaluation have not reached agreement on what standards should be used to judge personnel evaluation systems. While these professions have collaborated in developing standards for judging program evaluations, they have explicitly excluded the area of personnel evaluation (Joint Committee, 1981). Contributing to this avoidance is the fact that personnel evaluation provokes even more anxiety, controversy, and litigation than does program evaluation. Personnel evaluation is not an easy topic to address, and all parties, including professional educators and evaluators, have been quite happy to set it aside while they deal with more tractable topics. The state of the art in this area has remained stagnant for decades, and evaluation and school practitioners have not developed a sound working relationship on which to proceed cooperatively in such a controversial area. Consequently, the public and the professional education establishment have not had a professionally defined basis for judging educational personnel evaluation systems. By providing professional standards, this book is intended to fill that void.

Standards in Historical Perspective

Apart from the accreditation of schools movement that was launched in the late 1800s, there have been three major movements regarding educational evaluation in the United States. The first, which began and gained momentum in the early part of the twentieth century, was concerned with evaluation of student performance and was embodied primarily in the standardized testing movement. The second involved the evaluation of projects, especially externally funded projects, and was started in the middle 1960s. The third concerned evaluations of teachers

and other education personnel and has become a major movement only in recent years. The establishment of standards for
education evaluation work has paralleled these three major
developments in evaluation.

Standards in the area of student evaluation appeared first in
the 1950s in the form of *Standards for Educational and Psychological
Tests,* with three subsequent editions of those standards (NEA,
1955; APA, 1966, 1974, 1985). The *Standards for Evaluations of
Educational Programs, Projects, and Materials* were published in 1981
(Joint Committee on Standards for Educational Evaluation, 1981).
This book provides the first set of standards for evaluations of
educational personnel.

The sequence of these three movements and standard-setting
efforts is interesting. Obviously, the first concern in evaluating
an educational enterprise is the learning by its students. Hence,
it seems natural that the first attention to evaluation in education was focused on student performance, as reflected in the use
of standardized tests. If the resulting performance measures
revealed deficiencies in students' development, it is not surprising
that society and the profession of education would turn to the
evaluation of programs as one probable crucial reason for the
deficient performance.

That is precisely what happened in the middle 1960s when
the federal government became alarmed about the poor performance of disadvantaged children in the schools and recognized
the need for better educational programs in science and mathe-
matics. Massive federal efforts were undertaken to improve programs, along with a strong requirement that these programs be
evaluated. It is also true, and not surprising, that the program
evaluation movement of the late 1960s and early 1970s largely
excluded concern for the evaluation of the personnel who were
operating the programs and projects. Program evaluations proceeded on the assumption that deficiencies in programs were due
not to the personnel involved, but to the concepts and designs
of the programs. These assumptions were convenient and wel-
come, because they tended to minimize the threat inherent in
evaluation regarding accountability of individual teachers and
program personnel.

As continued evaluation of programs and students in the 1970s
and 1980s revealed further deficiencies in student performance
and program quality, pressure increased dramatically for focus-
ing accountability on individual educators. When professional
societies in education did not immediately respond, various state

education departments and school districts imposed new systems for personnel evaluation. The majority of states have enacted legislation requiring testing or other kinds of evaluation of teachers and other educators. The state systems for evaluating personnel have often been deficient, or at least controversial. While the logic of scrutinizing the qualifications of personnel when programs function poorly and students do not learn cannot be denied, educators have pointed to the hazards of hastily developed and poorly constructed personnel evaluation systems.

As a consequence, the professional societies in education have increased their efforts to develop sound personnel evaluation and, as one measure, fourteen of them are supporting the Joint Committee to develop standards by which to plan and assess personnel evaluations in schools and other educational agencies. The development of these standards provides a vital step toward helping the profession not only to improve personnel evaluation but to integrate that work effectively with other forms of evaluation, particularly of student needs and performance, program plans, operations, and outcomes.

The Development Process

These standards are the product of a process through which a large number of persons, representing the relevant perspectives, contributed collectively to defining shared principles for both guiding and assessing personnel evaluation work in education.

The first task during the first year of the project (1985) was to reach agreement on a structure and plan for developing and compiling the standards. The structure included an outline of the projected standards document, a list of issues to be converted into a first set of standards, and a format for writing possible versions of each standard. Subsequently, a national Panel of Writers, chosen largely through nominations by the sponsoring organizations, was established to produce the alternative versions. This initial stage of setting standards was completed when the full Committee finalized the structure and development plan, approved implementation, received the write-ups of each standard topic, evaluated the alternatives, and developed the first draft of *The Personnel Evaluation Standards* document.

The project staff submitted the first draft of *The Personnel Evaluation Standards* to the scrutiny of a National Review Panel and an International Review Panel in 1986. The panels included 78 persons nominated by the Sponsoring Organizations. Specifically, the panelists were asked to critique the first draft, applying a number of specified criteria, and to suggest improvements. The criteria included the following: need for the document; responsiveness to concerns in the field; scope of the standards; validity of their advice; practicality, political viability, legality, clarity, and depth of treatment; and appropriateness of language.

The project staff analyzed the critiques and reported the results to the Joint Committee at its July 1986 meeting. The Committee received a critique of its process and progress from the independent Validation Panel. The Committee then produced a second draft for field testing and for critique at national hearings. In the fall of 1986, the staff worked with the Joint Committee's Sponsoring Organizations to recruit individuals, institutions, and states to conduct field tests, participate in hearings, and provide critiques of the revised draft standards.

In 1987, the staff (a) scheduled and coordinated the hearings, field tests, and critiques; (b) analyzed the results; (c) developed a revised draft of this book; and obtained proposals from three publishing companies to publish *The Personnel Evaluation Standards*. Approximately thirty people presented testimony at hearings held during the spring in New Orleans, San Francisco, and Washington. Eighteen persons and groups submitted field test reports.

The Joint Committee met in July 1987 to make decisions for finalizing and publishing *The Personnel Evaluation Standards* and for dissemination activities. At that meeting, they received further reactions from the Validation Panel. Subsequently, the project staff proposed a final version of *The Personnel Evaluation Standards* to the full Committee for further modification and final approval.

After the Committee reached agreement on the finished form, they engaged the Validation Panel to evaluate and report publicly on the quality of *The Personnel Evaluation Standards*. Simultaneously, the publisher proceeded with the publishing process. Following publication, the Committee promoted *The Personel Evaluation Standards*, assisted education groups to use them, and set in motion a process of periodic review and revision.

The key participants in the development of the standards were as follows:

1. Joint Committee   The Joint Committee on Standards for Educational Evaluation was the primary decision-making board for this project. It functioned within its established policies and procedures (Joint Committee, 1981). The committee also (a) set additional policies, as needed, to govern the project; (b) approved main project documents (including funding proposals, *The Personnel Evaluation Standards*, and all Committee publications); (c) selected the membership of key panels; and (d) oversaw the activities of the project staff.

It is significant that the composition of the Committee satisfied a number of criteria. Among these were the following:

— Be appointed by a sponsoring organization or selected by the Committee as an at-large member, to a maximum of 19 members including the chair
— Represent a balance of viewpoints concerning both evaluation and education specializations
— Possess expertise for dealing with personnel evaluation as well as program evaluation
— Present a balance regarding race and gender

Perhaps the Committee's most important qualification was the diversity of viewpoints represented by its members, its sponsors, and the other groups with which it worked. Among others, these perspectives include those of school district superintendents, teachers, state government officials, school principals, personnel administrators, education psychologists, teacher educators, specialists in research on teaching, school board members, curriculum specialists, school counselors, evaluators, research methodologists, education lawyers, education policy researchers, philosophers, and testing experts. Through their work in developing the program evaluation standards, the Committee members learned to understand and respect each others' viewpoints, obtain other relevant views, and collaborate in finding areas of agreement.

2. Project Staff   The project was assisted by the following staff members at the Evaluation Center at Western Michigan University: Drs. Dale Brethower, Mary Ann Bunda, James Sanders, and Daniel Stufflebeam; Mrs. Linda Frisbie, Mrs. Sally Veeder, Ms. Sandra Ryan, Ms. Theresa Hollowell, Mrs. Mary Ramlow, Ms. Sue Vogel, Mr. Dennis Dressler, and the Department of Educational Leadership at Western Michigan University. Different persons were actively involved during different stages of the project; collectively, they are responsible for the large amount of staff work that was done.

3. The Sponsoring Organizations   The fourteen organizations that appointed members of the Joint Committee and helped define its charge continued to play an important role in this project. They provided a crucial communication link between the Committee and its constituents and assisted ongoing exchanges of information about the project by such activities as placing articles and news items in their journals and newsletters, sponsoring symposia and workshops at their conventions, and having project activities reported at their periodic board meetings. They nominated persons to serve on the panels. They were involved in setting up field tests, public hearings, and critiques. They also provided financial support for the travel costs associated with having their representatives attend the fall 1985, summer 1986, and summer 1987 meetings of the Joint Committee. Some of them contributed additional finances to help support the work of the Validation Panel.

4. The Validation Panel   The Validation Panel, chaired by Dr. Robert Linn, was commissioned to monitor the project and to examine the validity of *The Personnel Evaluation Standards*. The Panel's responsibilities were to identify and consider the assumptions underlying the project, to critique and report on the Joint Committee's validation process, to assess the applicability of *The Personnel Evaluation Standards* in various national and international contexts, to confront the Committee with issues and ideas drawn from pertinent theoretical analyses and empirical research reports, and to report publicly on their assessment of *The Personnel Evaluation Standards*. The members of the Panel were chosen to represent the following perspectives: personnel psychology, research on teaching, philosophy of education, international education, education law, education administration, and the teaching profession.

5. The Funding Agencies   Support for the project was provided by the following agencies: Lilly Endowment, Inc. ($89,000), Exxon Education Foundation ($50,000), Conrad N. Hilton Foundation ($50,000), Besser Foundation ($2,500), the Western Michigan University Foundation ($7,000), and several of the sponsoring organizations.

Personnel Evaluations
to Which the Standards Apply

Table 5 depicts the general evaluative context within which the standards apply. The table portrays personnel evaluation as an integral part of societal and institutional efforts to prepare, engage, and develop education personnel. The main horizontal dimension includes three systems called Preparation (e.g., teacher education), Practice (e.g., school teaching), and Continuing Education (e.g., study leaves and inservice education). The vertical dimension divides each system into Entry activities (e.g., selection of students for a principalship program), Participation (e.g., tenure reviews), and Exit (e.g., reduction in force decisions). The second horizontal dimension denotes Evaluations and Decisions that are involved in the Entry, Participation, and Exit stages of each personnel system.

The entries in the cells of the matrix reveal that a wide range of evaluations and decisions are involved in education personnel work. Moreover, the evaluations are of three different types. Some of them are program evaluations; e.g., evaluations of recruitment programs. Others, such as evaluations of students' mastery of college courses, are student evaluations. Finally, the great majority of the evaluations identified in the matrix fit the common view of personnel evaluation, i.e., assessments of the qualifications and performance of individual educators for certification, selection, tenure, staff development, and promotion.

The full range of evaluations depicted in the matrix are important to the effective staffing of education institutions, and all such evaluations should adhere to appropriate professional standards. Professional standards for student evaluations and program evaluations have existed for at least a decade, but there have been no standards focused specifically on education personnel evaluations.

This document is aimed at providing the standards needed to judge and improve the education personnel evaluations denoted in the matrix. Those evaluations and decisions on which these standards are primarily focused are provided in **bold type** letters. It is interesting and important that given categories of evaluation often provide information useful in making different decisions. This is especially the case for performance reviews that generate information for decisions about tenure, merit pay, promotion, and awards, as well as counseling for staff development. The standards require all parties to an evaluation to enter into the process with a clear idea of how the information to be collected will be used.

In the area of Preparation, the evaluations and decisions of most interest in these standards are those associated with selection of members of the profession. First, there are evaluations of applicants for particular preparation programs, such as teacher, counselor, and administrator education programs. A prime example is the system of assessment centers operated by the National Association of Secondary School Principals to assist in choosing and recruiting persons to enter graduate programs leading to employment as a high school principal. The second type of evaluation in the Preparation area are those done in the Exit stage to determine certification or licensing to practice. Evaluations of qualifications to practice are the evaluative bridge from the Preparations system to the Practice system.

As denoted by the **bold** entries under the Practice column, these standards apply most heavily to an institution's various evaluations of its staff members. Within the Entry stage, the standards apply most to evaluations of applicants for positions in teaching, administration, and other related roles. In the Participation stage of Practice, the standards concentrate on evaluations of job assignments and on performance reviews. The performance reviews are the most complex type of evaluation being addressed, since they provide information for such uses as deciding whether or not to continue probation; deciding about tenure, promotion, merit pay, honors, or recertification; and guidance on counseling for staff development. In the Exit stage of the Practice system, the standards are addressed to evaluations used to help decide on reduction in force, termination for cause, or withdrawal of licenses or certificates.

As seen under the third column, these standards are not directly addressed to evaluations in Continuing Education; the ones receiving primary attention in this realm are assessments of an individual staff member's needs or special qualifications to engage in some type of continuing education.

The evaluations and decisions identified in Table 1 are generic, and the Committee intends that the standards be applied broadly. Educational institutions of all types share a need for sound evaluations for entry into professional training, certifying competence, defining roles within the institution, selecting from job applicants, monitoring and providing feedback about performance, counseling for staff development, determining merit awards, and making decisions about tenure, promotion, and termination.

TABLE 5
Types of Evaluations and Decisions Involved in Preparing, Deploying, and Developing Professional Educators

Stages of Involvement	Educational Personnel Systems					
	PREPARATION		PRACTICE		CONTINUING EDUCATION	
	Evaluations	Decisions	Evaluations	Decisions	Evaluations	Decisions
	Evaluations of supply and demand	Assigning priorities and allocating funds to specialized training programs	Evaluations of staffing needs	Definitions of jobs Decisions to fill certain job vacancies	Correlated assessments of institutional and staff needs	Deciding on continuing education offerings/opportunities
ENTRY	Evaluations of recruitment programs	Determining how the programs should be changed or strengthened	Evaluations of recruitment programs	Determining how the programs should be changed or strengthened	*Assessments of the needs and achievements of individual staff members	*Deciding whether to approve applications for study leaves, sabbatical leaves, and for special grants
	*Assessments of applicants	*Selection of students	*Evaluations of applicants	*Selection of staff members	Intake evaluations	Designing individualized continuing education programs
	Intake Evaluations	Determining student programs	*Correlated evaluations of jobs and incumbents' qualifications	*Updating of job definitions	Progress reviews	Providing feedback to guide the learning process
PARTICIPATION	Evaluations of students' mastery of course requirements	Assigning course grades	*Reviews of job performance and special achievements	*Deciding whether to remove or continue probationary status or to terminate *Tenure *Promotion *Merit Pay *Counseling for staff development *Honors (awards) *Recertification		
	Cumulative progress reviews	Counseling for remediation Revising program plans Referrals to a termination review	Grievance hearings	Rulings on the grievances		

Final evaluations of students' fulfillment of their programs	Graduation decisions	*Correlated evaluations of finances, staffing needs, seniority of present staff and options for down-sizing	*Reduction in force decisions	Evaluations of participants' achievements in continuing education experiences	Deciding whether given applicants should be rewarded with future grants and/or leaves
*Evaluations of qualifications to practice given educational roles	*Certification *Licensing	*Evaluations of performance and/or investigations of charges	*Deciding whether to terminate *Deciding whether to withdraw licenses or certificates	Evaluations of qualifications to practice given educational roles	Certification Licensing New assignments

*Those evaluations and associated decisions which are of most concern in *The Evaluation of Standards*.

APPENDIX B

Citing the Standards

Users may wish publicly to cite the use of *The Personnel Evaluation Standards* as guiding the development, selection, application, or audit of an evaluation system. References to the use of *The Personnel Evaluation Standards* should not be made unless accompanied by statements of the extent to which the individual standards were considered.

A citation form that covers different levels of use and/or consideration of *The Personnel Evaluation Standards* is provided on the next page. This form provides a range of options for indicating the extent to which each standard was considered. Use of the form is recommended, and permission for users to reproduce the form is hereby granted. The form should be completed, signed, and attached to the evaluation plan, contract, or report.

Citation Form

The *Personnel Evaluation Standards* guided the development of this (check one):
  evaluation plan/design/proposal
  evaluation contract
  evaluation report
  other

To interpret the information provided on this form, the reader needs to refer to the full text of the *Standards*.

The *Standards* were consulted and used as indicated in the table below (check as appropriate):

	The Standard was deemed applicable and to the extent feasible was met	The Standard was deemed applicable but was not met	The Standard was not deemed applicable	Exception was taken to the Standard
P1 Service Orientation				
P2 Formal Evaluation Guidelines				
P3 Conflict of Interest				
P4 Access to Personnel Evaluation Reports				
P5 Interactions with Evaluatees				
U1 Constructive Orientation				
U2 Defined Uses				
U3 Evaluator Credibility				
U4 Functional Reporting				
U5 Follow-up and Impact				
F1 Practical Procedures				
F2 Political Viability				
F3 Fiscal Viability				
A1 Defined Role				
A2 Work Environment				
A3 Documentation of Procedures				—
A4 Valid Measurement				
A5 Reliable Measurement				
A6 Systematic Data Control				
A7 Bias Control				
A8 Monitoring Evaluation Systems				

Name: _____ Date: _____
          (typed)

_____
          (signature)
Position or Title: _____

Agency: _____

Address: _____

Relation to Document: _____
          (e.g., author of document, evaluation team leader,
          external auditor, internal auditor)

APPENDIX C

The Support Groups

Project Officers

The following persons reviewed proposals and reports and provided general administrative liaison between the funding agencies and the project:

William C. Bonifield (Lilly Endowment, Inc.)
H. Dean Evans (Lilly Endowment, Inc.)
Ellen Friedman (Conrad N. Hilton Foundation)
Russell Gabier (Western Michigan University Foundation)
Donald H. Hubbs (Conrad N. Hilton Foundation)
C. R. Reitz (Besser Foundation)
Robert Steiner (Conrad N. Hilton Foundation)

Project Staff

Dale Brethower
Mary Anne Bunda
Sharon Dodson
Dennis Dressler
Linda Frisbie
Michael Gagnon
Jean Heald
Theresa Hollowell
Sandra Ryan
James Sanders
Daniel Stufflebeam
Sally Veeder

Panel of Writers

Jane Bangert
Nashua, NH, School District

Marilyn Bittle
California Teachers Association

Dale Brethower
Department of Psychology
Western Michigan University

Esther Diamond
Private Consultant
Evanston, IL

Maurice Eash
College of Education
University of Illinois at Chicago

Laura Edwards
College of Education
University of Southwestern
   Louisiana

Mary Galloway
Delaware State Ed. Assn.

Richard Gazzola
Yonkers, NY Public Schools

Thomas Graham
Huber Heights, OH
Public Schools

Ethel Hines
Christina, DE, Public Schools

Jeremy Hughes
Haslett, MI, Public Schools

Ruben Ingram
Fountain Valley, CA
School District

Edward Iwanicki
School of Education
University of Connecticut

Rich Jacobs
Department of Psychology
Pennsylvania State University

Fran Jeffries
James Wood High School
Frederick County,
   Virginia Schools

Edgar A. Kelley
Department of Educational
   Leadership
Western Michigan University

Bernard McKenna
National Education Association

Robert McNergney
Research and Evaluation
   Department
University of Virginia

Donald Medley
School of Education
University of Virginia

Jason Millman
Educational Research
   Methodology
Cornell University

Bernard Oliver
Department of Health and
   Physical Education
Syracuse University

Sheila Pfafflin
AT&T

Sharon Rallis
Center for Evaluation and
   Research
Rhode Island College

Joan Regan
San Francisco, CA
Unified School System

Frances Robinson
Washington, DC
Public Schools

William Sedlacek
Counseling Center
University of Maryland

Robert Soar
College of Education
University of Florida

June Spooner
Dean Road Elementary School
Auburn, AL

Daniel Stufflebeam
Evaluation Center
Western Michigan University

Ross Traub
Department of Measurement
   and Evaluation
The Ontario Institute for
   Studies in Education

William Tullar
School of Business and
   Economics
University of North Carolina

Laura Wagner
Department of Education
State of California

General Consultants

Dale Brethower
Department of Psychology
Western Michigan University

Edgar A. Kelley
Department of Educational
   Leadership
Western Michigan University

Carol Norman
National Education Association

International Review Panel

David Andrich
Murdoch University
Western Australia

Simon Clyne
St. Patrick's College
Dublin, Ireland

Robert Conry
University of British Columbia
Canada

Janet G. Donald
Centre for University Teaching
   and Learning
Canada

Vincent Greaney
St. Patrick's College
Dublin, Ireland

David Hamilton
University of Glasgow
Scotland

Carol Heffernan
Patch American High School
West Germany

James Killeen, President
The World Confederation of
   Organization of the
   Teaching Profession
Canada

Ron Lane, President
Canadian School Trustees'
    Association

Ernest Lehmann
Verona School
Executive Director of Overseas
    Federation of Teachers

Tom Maguire
University of Alberta
Canada

Bob McGurrin
RAF Upper Heyford
England

Les McLean
Ontario Institute for Studies
    in Education

Gilles G. Nodeau
University of Moncton
Canada

Neville Postlethwaite
University of Hamburg
West Germany

G. A. Randell
University of Bradford
England

Marie Sainz-Funaro
Italy

Michael Scriven
University of Western Australia

Pinchas Tamir
Hebrew University
Israel

Ron Tickfer
HQ, USAE, AFCENT
Holland

D. Watkins
University of Canterbury
New Zealand

Ingemar Wedman
University of Umea
Sweden

C. H. Whitney
Executive Director
Canadian School Trustees'
    Association

Jac Zaal
Rijks Psychologishe Dienst
The Netherlands

National Review Panel

Nelson Ashline
IL State Board of Educators

Sue Bentz
IL State Board of Educators

Leonard Bickman
Vanderbilt University

James Blank, President
Wisconsin Education
    Association Council

Gwyneth Boodoo
Texas A&M University

David Brauhn
Prairie Intermediate School

John Cole
Texas Federation President

John Coleman
Beverly, MA

Donna Cox
Elementary Principal
Springfield R12 School Dist.

Cory Cummings
Florida State University

Raymond E. Curry
Assoc. of CA School Admin.

Gay Nelle Estes
Montgomery, AL

Gerry Firth
University of Georgia

Antoine Garibaldi
Xavier University

Gladys Graves
President
NC Association of Educators

LaBarbara Gregg
Detroit Public Schools

Ann Gregory
St. Paul, VA

Gene Hall
University of Texas—Austin

Bob Hanes, Administrator
Charlotte-Mecklenburg
    Public Schools

Alice Harden, President
MS Association of Education

Ben Harris
University of Texas

Walter E. Hathaway
Portland Public Schools

Ernest House
University of Colorado

Kenneth R. Howe
Michigan State University

Lloyd G. Humphries
University of Illinois

Mack Irving
Ozark, AL

M. Claradine Johnson
Wichita State University

Mildred E. Katzell
Glen Cove, NY

A. S. Kramer
VA Medical Center

Nat LaCour, President
United Teacher Association of
    New Orleans

Donald Langlois
Lehigh University

Dal Lawrence, President
Toledo Federation of Teachers

David Lepard
George Mason University

Dick Manatt
Iowa State University

Donald McCarty
University of Wisconsin

William G. Monahan
West Virginia University

Margaret Mueller
Trenton, NJ

Tony Nitko
University of Pittsburgh

John Ory
University of Illinois

Maureen Peters
Dallas, TX

Stuart Rankin
Detroit Public Schools

Frank Rapley
Kalamazoo, MI, Public Schools

Wayne Robbins
Confederation of Oregon
    School Administrators

Carol Robinson
Albuquerque Public Schools

Carroll R. Sawin
Lincoln Public Schools

Signa Segrist, President
Houston Teachers

Calla Smorodin
NJ State Department
    of Education

Louise Sundin
Minneapolis, MN

Carol Tittle
City College of New York

Millie Wallace
Papillion, NV

Richard Wallace
Pittsburgh Public Schools

Reg Weaver, President
Illinois Education Association

Hilda Wing
Psychological Corporation

Linus Wright
Dallas Independent School
    District

Validation Panel

Chair
Robert Linn, University of Colorado

Members
Margret Buchmann, Michigan State University
Bruce Gould, Brooks Air Force Base, Texas
Thomas Kellaghan, St. Patrick's College, Dublin, Ireland
Dal Lawrence, Toledo Federation of Teachers
Phil Robinson, Clarence B. Sabbath School, River Rouge
Perry Zirkel, Lehigh University

Field Test Participants

Dale M. Brethower, Michigan
Richard A. Gorton, Wisconsin

Joseph V. Grebb, Virginia
David Holdzkom, North Carolina
Ann V. Kraetzer, Colorado
James S. Long, Washington
Kathleen B. Lynch, Virginia
C. Benjamin Meleca, Ohio
C. Rebecca Montoya, Illinois
Carol Norman, Washington, DC
James A. Pearsol, Ohio
William Quinn, Utah
A. M. Srikanta Rao, Alabama
Robert A. Reineke, Nebraska
David L. Sanger, Michigan
Carrol Sawin, Nebraska
Lowell K. Scott, Kentucky
Don Soderberg, Vermont
Dennis C. Stacey, North Carolina
Thomas Truitt, Virginia
Charles E. Warfield, Michigan
Marjorie J. Willeke, Nebraska

Hearings Participants

New Orleans
Renee Casbergue, Louisiana
William D'Amour, Minnesota
Carl Glickman, Georgia
Robert King, New York
Robert Lerch, Idaho
Gerald Reece, New Mexico
Gina Schack, Louisiana
Ralph Tyler, California

San Francisco
Eva Bacal, Arizona
Frank Barham, Virginia
Hugh Broadus, Montana
David Geiger, Oregon
JoAnn Kellogg, Louisiana
Martha Miller, Kansas
Joseph Zemaitis, New Jersey

Washington, DC
J. Bradley Cousins, Canada
Donald Dunbar, Pennsylvania
Pascal Forgione, Connecticut
John Fremer, Texas
Kenneth Leithwood, Canada
John Poggio, Kansas
W. James Popham, California
Andrew Porter, Michigan
Larry Skurnick, Colorado

Editors

Philip S. Denenfeld
Daniel L. Stufflebeam

GLOSSARY

The terms in this glossary are defined as they are used in this volume, in the context of evaluation. In other settings, a number of them may have different or less specialized definitions.

Accuracy   The extent to which an evaluation conveys technically adequate information about the performance and qualifications of an evaluatee.

Administration   Management of an organization through such actions as planning, staffing, motivating, directing, controlling, communicating, and evaluating.

Affective dimension   The psychological element consisting of a person's feelings, emotions, or degree of acceptance or rejection of an object, concept, or experience.

Anonymity (provision for)   Evaluator action to ensure that the identity of involved individuals cannot be ascertained during the course of a study or in study reports.

Assessment   The act of rating or describing a subject on some variable of interest.

Assessment center   A process (not a location) employing simulation techniques to identify and measure a wide variety of administrative job skills. Most centers are designed to identify or select individuals for advancement into or within management. The assessees participate in a number of activities that simulate behaviors typically found in management or administrative positions.

Assessment procedure   Any method used to rate or describe some characteristic of a subject.

Attribute   A characteristic or quality seen as possessed by a person.

Audiences   Those persons to be guided by the results of an evaluation in making decisions, and all others with a stake in the evaluation.

Audit (of an evaluation)   An independent examination and verification of the quality of an evaluation plan, the adequacy of its implementation, the accuracy of results, and the validity of conclusions.

Battery   A combination of two or more instruments or procedures.

Behavior   Specific, observable actions of an individual in response to internal and external stimuli.

Behavioral terms   Descriptions of human qualifications or performance expressed as objective, accessible facts of a person's behavior.

Benefit   An advantageous consequence of a program or action.

Bias   Any constant error; any systematic influence on measures or on statistical results irrelevant to the purpose of measurement.

Career ladder scale   An incremental pay scale through which a teacher advances as a result of favorable evaluations.

Client   The individual, group, or organization that employs the evaluator; persons who receive or benefit from education services, such as students and parents.

Code (information)   To translate a given set of data or items into a set of quantitative or qualitative symbols.

Coefficient   A value expressing the degree to which some characteristic or relation exists in specified instances; e.g., the coefficient of correlation is a value expressing the degree to which two variables vary concomitantly.

Cognitive ability   The psychological element consisting of such mental processes as perceiving, knowing, recognizing, conceptualizing, judging, and reasoning.

Competency   A skill, knowledge, or experience that is suitable or sufficient for some purpose.

Conclusions (of an evaluation)   Final judgments and recommendations.

Conflict of interest   A situation in which an evaluator's private interests affect her or his evaluative actions, or in which the evaluative actions might affect private interests.

Construct   A characteristic or trait of individuals inferred from empirical evidence (e.g., numerical ability).

Contamination   Any systematic influence on measures or on statistical results irrelevant to the purpose of measurement; any bias or error.

Content domain   A body of knowledge and/or a set of tasks or other behaviors defined so that given facts or behaviors may be classified as included or excluded.

Context   The set of circumstances or acts that surround and may affect a particular job, situation, etc.

Contextual variables   Indicators or dimensions that are useful in describing the facts or circumstances that surround a particular job situation and influence a person's performance on that job.

Contract   A written or oral agreement between any two parties that describes a mutual understanding of expectations and responsibilities for both parties.

Correlation The degree to which two or more sets of measurements vary together; e.g., a positive correlation exists when high values on one scale are associated with high values on another.

Cost effectiveness The extent to which one program, project, or instructional material produces equal or better results than competitors in time, effort, and resources; or the extent to which an object produces the same results as competitors but is less costly.

Credibility Worthy of belief or confidence by virtue of being trustworthy and possessing pertinent knowledge, skills, and experience.

Criterion A measure of job performance, such as productivity, accident rate, absenteeism, reject rate, or training score. It also includes subjective measures such as supervisory ratings.

Criterion-referenced tests Tests whose scores are interpreted by referral to specifically defined performances, rather than to the performance of some comparable group of people.

Critical score A specified point in a predictor distribution of scores below which candidates are rejected.

Cross validation The application of a scoring system or set of weights empirically derived in one sample to a different sample (drawn from the same population) to investigate the stability of relationships based on the original weights.

Data Material gathered during the course of an evaluation which serves as the basis for information, discussion, and inference.

Data access The extent to which an evaluator will be permitted to obtain data during the course of an evaluation.

Data analysis The process of studying data to arrive at answers to questions.

Data collection procedures Any set of steps used to obtain quantitative or qualitative information about the qualifications or performance of an individual.

Dependent variable A measure (e.g., a student's performance on a test) that is assumed to vary as a result of some influence (often taken to be the independent variable), such as a student's instructional experience.

Derived score A scale of measurement using a system of standard units (based perhaps on standard deviations or centiles) to which obtained scores on any original scale may be transformed by appropriate numerical manipulation.

Design (evaluation) A representation of the set of decisions that determine how an evaluation is to be conducted; e.g., data collection schedule, report schedules, questions to be addressed, analysis plan, management plan, etc. Designs may be either preordinate or emergent.

Evaluatee The person whose qualifications or performance is evaluated.

Evaluation Systematic investigation of the worth or merit of something; e.g., a person's qualifications or performance in a given role.

Evaluation system A regularized structure and set of procedures by which an institution initiates, designs, implements, and uses evaluations of its personnel or programs.

Evaluator Anyone who accepts and executes responsibility for planning, conducting, and reporting evaluations.

Expectancy table A table or chart used for predicting levels of criterion performance for specified intervals of predictor scores.

External evaluation Evaluation conducted by an evaluator from outside the organization housing the object of the study.

External referent group A body of persons outside an individual's immediate work environment whose aims and standards he or she is bound to serve and honor because of membership in the group; e.g., the scientific community, professional teachers, educational administrators, or evaluators.

Extrapolate To infer an unknown from something known. (Statistical definition—to estimate the value of a variable outside its observed range.)

Feasibility The extent to which an evaluation is appropriate and practical for implementation.

Field test The study of a program, project, or instructional material in a setting like those where it is to be used. Field tests may range from preliminary primitive investigations to full-scale summative studies.

Formative evaluation Evaluation conducted while a creative process is under way, designed and used to promote growth and improvement in a person's performance or in a program's development.

Gain scores The difference between a person's performance on a test and his or her performance on a subsequent administration of the same test.

Generalizability The extent to which information collected in one setting about a program, project, or instructional material can be used to reach a valid prediction of its utility and reliability in other settings.

Incentive pay Compensation paid to employees for doing different *kinds* or *amounts* or work. Incentive pay plans may open new opportunities for professional development, or they may increase the volume of work tasks. Although some such plans require that employees be judged meritorious in order to participate, incentive pay differs from merit pay.

Informed consent Agreement by the participants in an evaluation that their names and/or confidential information supplied by them may be used in specified ways, for stated purposes, and in light of possible consequences prior to the collection and/or release of this information in evaluation reports.

Instrument   An assessment device adopted, adapted, or constructed for the purposes of the evaluation.

Internal evaluation   Evaluation conducted by a staff member from within the organization in which the evaluation is occurring.

Internal referent   A body of persons within an individual's work group environment with whom he or she interacts because of similar interests, complementary skills, common professional allegiances, collaborative assignments, etc.

Job analysis   A method of analyzing jobs in terms of the tasks performed; the performance standards and training content; and the required knowledge, skills, and abilities.

Level of significance   A predetermined probability value used to decide whether the results occurred by chance.

Linear combination   The sum of scores (whether weighted differentially or not) on different assessments to form a single composite score. (Distinguished from nonlinear combinations, in which the different scores may, for example, be multiplied instead of added.)

Longevity pay   Pay increases based solely on accrued length of service.

Master teacher   A teacher recognized for superior ability and performance. Master teacher plans generally enable career advancement and development through the assignment of new duties, such as curriculum development, supervision and coaching of new faculty members, teaching special classes for gifted students, or other leadership roles.

Mean (arithmetic)   The average of a set of numbers.

Merit   Excellence as assessed by intrinsic qualities or performance.

Merit pay   Monetary compensation in the form of higher wages or salaries awarded to deserving employees—who may have the same job descriptions and responsibilities as other employees not receiving merit pay—on the basis of verifiable superiority in the *quality* of their work performance. The differences in compensation, which may be one-time bonuses or permanent pay increases, are usually based on annual systematic evaluations of employee performance.

Norm   A single value, or a distribution of values, constituting the typical performance of a given group.

Objective evaluation   Evaluation carried out in a way that minimizes error or bias due to the predilections of the evaluator.

Operational definition   A definition of a construct or object stating the operations or procedures employed to measure it.

Operational independence   Gathering of data by methods that are different in procedure or source, so that measurement of one variable, such as a criterion, is not influenced by the process of measuring another variable.

Opportunity cost A giving up of one's option to use a situation or condition favorable to attaining a goal in order to engage in a particular activity.

Parallel forms Multiple forms of a test constructed to be as comparable and interchangeable as possible in their content, difficulty, length, and administration procedures, and in the scores and test properties (e.g., means, reliability indices, etc.).

Performance standard A formal specification of the expected level of achievement in fulfilling a performance objective.

Personnel evaluation The systematic assessment of a person's performance and/or qualifications in relation to a role and some specified, defensible institutional purpose.

Personnel evaluation system All of the rules, procedures, assignments, and other elements that an institution uses to evaluate its personnel.

Pilot test A brief, simplified preliminary trial study designed to learn whether a proposed project or program seems likely to yield valuable results.

Post-test A test to assess performance after the administration of a program, project, or instructional material.

Pre-test A test to assess performance prior to the administration of a program, project, or instructional material.

Predictor A measurable characteristic used to predict criterion performance; e.g., scores on a test or the judgments of interviewers.

Propriety The extent to which an evaluation will be conducted legally, ethically, and with due regard for the welfare of those involved in the evaluation as well as those affected by its results.

Psychometric Pertaining to the measurement of psychological characteristics, such as aptitudes, personality traits, achievement, skill, and knowledge.

Qualitative information Facts and claims presented in narrative, not numerical, form.

Quantitative information Facts and claims represented by numbers.

Random sampling Drawing a number of items of any sort from a larger group or population, so that every individual item has the same (and independent) chance as any other to be chosen.

Replication A repetition of a study intended to investigate the generalizability or stability of the results.

Role definition Specification of the behavior that is characteristic and expected of the occupant of a defined position in a group.

Sample A part of a population.

School district   A legally constituted collection of institutions, within defined geographic boundaries, that collaborate in teaching persons under college age.

Score   Any specific value in a range of possible values describing the assessment of an individual.

Self-report instrument   A device in which persons make and report judgments about their own performance.

Significant difference (statistically)   An observed difference between two statistics that probably did not occur by chance.

Standard   A principle commonly agreed to by experts in the conduct and use of evaluation by which to measure the value or quality of an evaluation.

Standard score   A score that describes the location of a person's score within a set of scores in terms of distance from the mean in standard deviation units; it may include scores on certain derived scales.

Standardized test   A set of items or situations with definite directions for administration and scoring, usually accompanied by data on reliability and validity and sometimes by normative information.

Statistic   A summary number used typically to describe a characteristic of a sample.

Subjective evaluation   An evaluation not open to verification by others not using public or communicable standards.

Summative evaluation   Evaluation designed to present conclusions about the merit or worth of a person's performance.

Utility   The extent to which an evaluation will serve the relevant information needs of evaluatees and other users.

Variable   A characteristic that can take on different values.

INDEXES

A: Roles in Illustrative Cases

B: Institutions in Cases

C: Purposes in Cases

D: Personnel Actions in Cases

E: Subject Index

INDEX A

Roles in Illustrative Cases

INDEX B

Institutions in Illustrative Cases

INDEX C

Purposes in Illustrative Cases

INDEX D

Personnel Actions in Illustrative Cases

INDEX E

Subject Index

BIBLIOGRAPHY

Acheson, K., & Gall, M. (1980). *Techniques in the clinical supervision of teachers*. New York: Longman.

American Association of School Administrators. (1978). *Standards for school personnel administration* (3rd ed.). Seven Hills, OH: Author.

American Educational Research Association/American Psychological Association/National Council on Measurements Used in Education. (1985). *Standards for educational and psychological tests*. Washington, DC: Author.

American Educational Research Association and National Council on Measurements Used in Education. (1955). *Technical recommendations for achievement tests*. Washington, DC: National Education Association.

American Psychological Association. (1966). *Standards for educational and psychological tests and manuals*. Washington, DC: Author.

American Psychological Association. (1974). *Standards for educational and psychological tests* (rev. ed.). Washington, DC: Author.

American Psychological Association, Division 14. (1980). *Principles for the validation and use of personnel selection procedures*. Washington, DC: Author.

Anderson, S., Bell, S., Murphy, R., & associates. (1975). *Encyclopedia of educational evaluation: Concepts and techniques for evaluating education and training programs*. San Francisco: Jossey-Bass.

Andrews, H. A. (1985). *Evaluating for excellence*. Stillwater, OK: New Forums.

Bacharach, S. B., Lipsky, D. B., & Shedd, J. B. (1984). *Paying for better teaching: Merit pay and its alternatives*. Ithaca, NY: Organizational Analysis and Practice, Inc.

Barber, T. X. (1976). *Pitfalls in human research: Ten pivotal points*. New York: Pergamon.

Bartko, J. J. (1976). On various intraclass reliability coefficients. *Psychological Bulletin, 83*, 762-765.

Bellon, J. J. (1984). Evaluator competencies needed for evaluating teachers and teaching. *Thresholds in Education, 10*, 22-24.

Bernardin, H. J., & Beatty, R. W. (1984). *Performance appraisal: Assessing human behavior at work*. Boston: Kent.

Biles, B. L. (1982). *Training and resource manual: Educational research and dissemination program*. Washington, DC: American Federation of Teachers.

Block, J. R. (1981). *Performance appraisal on the job: Making it work*. New York: Prentice-Hall.

Blumberg, A. (1980). *Supervisors and teachers: A private cold war.* Berkeley, CA: McCutchan.

Bolton, D. L. (1973). *Selection and evaluation of teachers.* Berkeley, CA: McCutchan.

Bolton, D. L. (1980). *Evaluating administrative personnel in school systems.* New York: Teachers College Press.

Booth, R. R., & Glaub, G. R. (1978). *Planned appraisal of the superintendent.* Springfield: Illinois Association of School Boards.

Boyer, E. L. (1983). *High school.* New York: Harper & Row.

Brock, S. C. (1981). Evaluation-based teacher development. In J. Millman (Ed.), *Handbook of teacher evaluation.* Beverly Hills, CA: Sage.

Brodinsky, B. (1984). Teacher morale: What builds it, what kills it. *Education Digest, 50*(3), 12-15.

Brophy, J., & Good, T. L. (1986). Teacher behavior and student achievement. In M. Wittrock (Ed.), *Third handbook of research on teaching.* New York: Macmillan.

Brown, A. F., Rix, E. A., & Cholvat, J. (1983). Changing promotion criteria: Cognitive effects on administrators' decisions. *Journal of Experimental Education, 52,* 4-10.

Carnegie Task Force on Teaching as a Profession. (1986). *A nation prepared: Teachers for the 21st century.* Hyattsville, MD: Carnegie Forum on Education and the Economy.

Carroll, S. J., & Schneier, C. E. (1982). *Performance appraisal and review systems: The identification measurement, and development of performance in organizations.* Glenview, IL: Scott, Foresman.

Cascio, W. F. (1982). *Applied psychology in personnel management.* Reston, VA: Reston.

Cascio, W. F., & Silbey, V. (1979). Utility of the assessment center as a selection device. *Journal of Applied Psychology, 64,* 107-118.

Castetter, W. B. (1981). *The personnel function in educational administration* (3rd ed.). New York: Macmillan.

Centra, J. A. (1982). *Determining faculty effectiveness.* San Francisco: Jossey-Bass.

Christina School District, Newark, DE. (1984). *Personnel services handbook.* Unpublished handbook.

Christina School District, Newark, DE. (1986). *Agreement between the Christina School District Board of Education and the Christina Education Association, Inc.* Unpublished handbook.

Coker, H., Medley, D., & Soar, R. (1980). How valid are expert opinions about effective teaching. *Phi Delta Kappan, 62,* 131-134.

Committee to Develop Standards for Educational and Psychological Testing. (1985). *Standards for educational and psychological tests.* Washington, DC: American Psychological Association.

Cooper, W. H. (1981). Ubiquitous halo. *Psychological Bulletin, 90,* 218-244.

Darling-Hammond, L., Wise, A. E., & Peace, S. R. (1983). Teacher evaluation in the organization context: A review of the literature. *Review of Educational Research, 53,* 285-328.

Davis, B., & Arnof, D. (1983). *How to fix what's wrong with our schools.* New Haven: Ticknor & Fields.

Doyle, K. O. (1983). *Evaluative teaching.* Lexington, MA: Lexington Books.

Duckett, W. R. (n.d.). (Ed.). *Planning for the evaluation of teaching.* Bloomington, IN: Phi Delta Kappa.

Duke, D. L., & Stiggins, R. J. (1986). *Teacher evaluation* [A joint publication of American Association of School Administrators, National Association of Elementary School Principals, National Association of Secondary School Principals, and National Education Association]. Washington, DC: National Education Association.

Educational Research Service, Inc. (1974). *Evaluating administrative performance.* Arlington, VA: Educational Research Service.

Emmer, E. T. et al. (1982). *Organizing and managing the junior high classroom.* Austin: University of Texas.

Evertson, C. M., & Holley, F. M. (1981). Classroom observation. In J. Millman (Ed.), *Handbook of teacher evaluation.* Beverly Hills, CA: Sage.

Fletcher, C. (1984, February). What's new in performance appraisal? *Personnel Management,* pp. 20-22.

Fox, T. G., & Egan, K. B. (1982). *Teacher evaluation: A critical review of their purposes and practices.* Paper presented at the Annual Meeting of the American Educational Research Association, New York.

French-Lazovik, G. (Ed.). (1982). *Practices that improve teaching evaluation.* San Francisco: Jossey-Bass.

Frick, T., & Semmel, M. I. (1978). Observer agreement and reliabilities of classroom observational measures. *Review of Educational Research, 1,* 157-184.

Furtwengler, C., McLarty, J., & Malo, G. (1985, April). *The career ladder program in Tennessee.* Presented at the Annual Meeting of the National Council on Measurement in Education, Chicago.

Genck, F. (1983). *Improving school performance.* New York: Praeger.

Ghorpade, J., & Atchison, T. J. (1980, Fall). The concept of job analysis: A review and some suggestions. *Public Personnel Management Journal,* pp. 134-144.

Glasman, N. S. (n.d.). The school principal as evaluator, Midwest Administrative Center, University of Chicago. *Administrator's Notebook, 31*(2).

Goodlad, J. I. (1983). *A place called school.* New York: McGraw-Hill.

Gorton, R. A. (1976). *School administration: Challenge and opportunity for leadership.* Dubuque, IA: William C Brown.

Greller, M. M., & Herold, D. M. (1975). Sources of feedback: A preliminary investigation. *Organizational Behavior and Human Performance, 13,* 244-256.

Grossnickle, D., & Cutter, T. (1984). It takes one to know one—advocating colleagues as evaluators. *NASSP Bulletin,* pp. 56-60.

Guion, R. M. (1961). Criterion measurement and personnel judgment. *Personnel Psychology, 14,* 141-149.

Haetele, D. (1980). How to evaluate the teacher—let me count the ways. *Phi Delta Kappan*, pp. 312-349.

Harris, B. M. (1986). Linkages to summative awards and termination. Chapter 10 in *Developmental teacher evaluation*. Boston: Allyn & Bacon.

Henderson, R. (1981). *Performance appraisal: Theory to practice*. Reston, VA: Reston.

Heneman, H. G., Schwab, D. P., Fossum, J. A., & Dyer, L. D. (1983). *Personnel/human resource management*. Homewood, IL: Richard D. Irwin.

Hersey, P. W. (1987). *How NASSP helps identify, develop superior principals*. Reston, VA: National Association of Secondary School Principals.

Howard, A. (1974). 18. An assessment of assessment centers. *Academy of Management Journal*, 74, 115-34.

Hunter, M. (1979). Teaching is decision making. *Educational Leadership*, 37, 408-412.

Hunter, M. (1983). *Mastery teaching*. El Segundo, CA: Tip Publications.

Imundo, L. V. (1980). *The effective supervisor's handbook*. New York: AMACOM—American Management Associations.

Iwanicki, E. F. (1981). Development and validation of the teacher evaluation needs identification survey. *Educational and Psychological Measurement*, 42, 265-274.

Jacobs, R., Kafry, D., & Zedreck, S. (1980). Expectations of behaviorally anchored rating scales. *Personnel Psychology*, 33, 595-640.

Johnson, M. (1982). *A summary of court cases involving termination of tenured faculty members*. Unpublished graduate research project, Illinois Valley Community College, Ogelsby.

Johnson, S. (1980). Performance-based staff layoffs in the public schools: Implementation and outcomes. *Harvard Educational Review*, 50, 214-233.

Joint Committee on Standards for Educational Evaluation. (1981). *Standards for evaluations of educational programs, projects, and materials*. New York: McGraw-Hill.

Kahalas, H. (1980). The environmental context of performance evaluation and its effect on current practices. *Human Resource Management*, 19, 32-40.

Kane, J. S., & Lawler, E. (1979). Performance appraisal effectiveness: Its assessment and determinants. In I. B. Straw (Ed.), *Research in organizational behavior* (Vol. 1). Greenwich, CT: JAI Press.

Kaye, B. L. (1982). *Up is not the only way: A guide for career development practitioners*. Englewood Cliffs, NJ: Prentice-Hall.

Lacho, K. J., Stearns, G. K., & Billere, M. F. (1979). A study of employee appraisal systems of major cities in the U.S. *Pupil Personnel Management*, 8, 111-125.

Landy, F. J., Barnes-Farell, J. L., & Cleveland, J. N. (1980). Perceived fairness and accuracy of performance evaluation: A follow-up. *Journal of Applied Psychology*, 65, 355-356.

Landy, F. J., Barnes, J. L., & Murphy, K. R. (1978). Correlates of perceived fairness and accuracy of performance evaluation. *Journal of Applied Psychology, 63,* 751-754.

Landy, F. J., & Farr, J. L. (1980). Performance rating. *Psychological Bulletin, 87,* 72-107.

Landy, F. J., & Farr, J. L. (1983). *The measurement of work performance: Methods, theory, and applications.* New York: Academic Press.

Lee, R. D., Jr. (1979). *Public personnel systems.* Baltimore: University Park Press.

Locher, A. H., & Teel, K. S. (1977). Performance appraisal: A survey of current practices. *Personnel Journal, 56,* 245-254.

Manasse, A. L. (1984). *A policymaker's guide to improving conditions for principals' effectiveness.* Alexandria, VA: National Association of State Boards of Education.

Manatt, R. P., Palmer, K. L., & Hidlebaugh, E. (1976). Evaluating teaching performance with improved rating scales. *NASSP Bulletin, 60,* 21-23.

McGaw, G., Wardrop, J. L., & Bunda, M. A. (1972). Classroom observational schemes: Where are the errors? *American Educational Research Journal, 9,* 13-17.

McGreal, T. L. (1981). *Successful teacher evaluation* [Published in cooperation with the National Council on Measurement in Education]. Beverly Hills, CA: Sage.

McGreal, T. L. (1982). Effective teacher evaluation systems. *Educational Leadership, 39,* 303-305.

McKenna, B. H. (1981). Criteria of good teaching. In J. Millman (Ed.), *Handbook of teacher evaluation.* Beverly Hills, CA: Sage.

McNeil, J., & Popham, W. J. (1973). The assessment of teacher competence. In R. M. W. Travers (Ed.), *Second handbook of research on teaching.* Chicago: Rand McNally.

McNergney, R., & Carrier, C. (1981). *Teacher development.* New York: Macmillan.

Medley, D. M., Coker, H., & Soar, R. S. (1984). *Measurement-based evaluation of teacher performance: An empirical approach.* New York: Longman.

Millman, J. (Ed.). (1981). *Handbook of teacher evaluation.* Beverly Hills, CA: Sage.

Morris, V. C., & Pai, Y. (1976). *Philosophy and the American school.* Boston: Houghton Mifflin.

Morrison, J., & O'Hearne, J. (1977). *Practical transactional analysis in management.* Reading, MA: Addison-Wesley.

Moses, J. L., & Ritchie, R. J. (1976). Supervisory relationships training: A behavioral evaluation of a behavior modeling program. *Personnel Psychology, 29,* 337-343.

National Association of Elementary School Principals. (1986). *Proficiencies for principals.* Alexandria, VA: Author.

National Commission on Excellence in Education. (1983). *A nation at at risk: The imperative of educational reform.* Washington, DC: Government Printing Office. (No. 065-000-00177-2).

National Science Foundation. (1983). *Educating Americans for the 21st century*. Washington, DC: Author.

Neagley, R., & Evans, N. D. (1980). *Supervision of instruction* (2nd ed.). Englewood Cliffs, NJ: Prentice-Hall.

NEA. (1955). *Standards for educational and psychological tests*. Washington, DC: Author.

NEA Position Paper. (1983). *The N.E.A. on master teacher/merit pay plans*. Washington, DC: National Education Association.

O'Dell, C. (1985). *The ABC's of teacher evaluation*. Yreka, CA: Mardell.

Oliver, B. (1982). Desirable qualities in teacher performance appraisal systems. *Teacher Educator, 18*, 26-30.

Patten, T. H., Jr. (1982). *A manager's guide to performance appraisal*. New York: Free Press.

Peterson, K. (1984). Methodological problems in teacher evaluation. *Journal of Research and Development in Education, 17*, 62-70.

Peterson, P. E. (1983). *Making the grade*. New York: Twentieth Century Fund Task Force on Federal Elementary and Secondary Education Policy.

Poliakoff, L. L. (1973). *Evaluating school personnel today*. Washington, DC: ERIC Clearinghouse on Teacher Education (No. ED 073 045).

Popham, W. J. (1975). Contemporary conceptions of educational evaluation. In *Educational evaluation*. Englewood Cliffs, NJ: Prentice-Hall.

Pugach, M. C., & Rath, J. C. (1983). Testing teachers: Analysis and recommendations. *Journal of Teacher Education, 34*, 37-43.

Redfern, G. B. (1980). *Evaluating teachers and administrators: A performance objectives approach*. Boulder, CO: Westview Press.

Robertson, M. J. (1973). *Personnel evaluation in vocational and technical education*. Columbus: Ohio State University Center for Vocational and Technical Education.

Rood, H. J. (1977). Legal issues in faculty termination: An analysis on recent court cases. *Journal of Higher Education, 48*, 123-149.

Rossi, P. H., & Freeman, H. E. (1982). *Evaluation: A systematic approach*. Beverly Hills, CA: Sage.

Rowley, G. L. (1976). Reliability of observational measures. *American Education Research Journal, 13*, 51-59.

Schmitt, N., Noe, R., Merritt, R., Fitzgerald, M., & Jorgensen, C. (n.d.). *Criterion-related and content validity of the NASSP assessment center*. East Lansing: Michigan State University.

Scriven, M. (1983). Evaluation ideologies. In G. Madaus, M. Scriven, & D. Stufflebeam (Eds.), *Evaluation models: Viewpoints on educational and human service evaluation*. Boston: Kluwer-Nijhoff.

Seldin, P. (1984). *Changing practices in faculty evaluation*. San Francisco: Jossey-Bass.

Sergiovanni, T. J. (1982). Toward a theory of supervisory practice: Integrating scientific, clinical, and artistic views. In T. J. Sergiovanni (Ed.), *Supervision of teaching* (pp. 67-78). Alexandria, VA: Association for Supervision and Curriculum Development.

Sergiovanni, T. J. (1984). Expanding conceptions of inquiry and practice in supervision and evaluation. *Educational Evaluation and Policy Analysis, 6,* 355-365.

Smith, H. P., & Brouwer, P. J. (1977). *Performance appraisal and human development.* Reading, MA: Addison-Wesley.

Smith, P. C. (1976). Behavior, results, and organizational effectiveness: The problems of criteria. In M. D. Dunnette (Ed.), *Handbook of industrial and organizational psychology.* Chicago: Rand McNally.

Soar, R. S., Medley, D. M., & Coker, H. (1983). Teacher evaluation: A critique of currently used methods. *Phi Delta Kappan, 65,* 239-246.

Stow, S. B., & Manatt, R. P. (1982, February). Administrator evaluation tailored to your district or independent school. *Educational Leadership,* pp. 353-356.

Strike, K., & Bull, B. (1981). Fairness and the legal context of teacher evaluation. In J. Millman (Ed.), *Handbook of teacher evaluation* (pp. 303-343), National Council on Measurement in Education. Beverly Hills, CA: Sage.

Stufflebeam, D. L., & Brethower, D. M. (1987). Improving personnel evaluations through professional standards. *Journal of Personnel Evaluation in Education, 1,* 125-155.

Task Force on Assessment Center Standards. (1979, June). *Standards and ethical considerations for assessment center operations* [Endorsed by the 7th International Conference on Assessment Center Method, New Orleans].

Thorndike, R. L., & Hagen, E. (1977). *Measurement and evaluation in psychology and education.* New York: John Wiley.

Thornton, G., & Byham, W. (1982). *Assessment centers and managerial performance.* New York: Academic Press.

Travers, R. M. W. (1981). Criteria of good teaching. In J. Millman (Ed.), *Handbook of teacher evaluation.* Beverly Hills, CA: Sage.

Tullar, W. L., & Mullins, T. W. (1985, June). Performance appraisal as an organizational intervention: A case study of appraisals as a unifier of corporate cultures. *American Business Review.*

Webb, L. D. (1983). *Teacher evaluation.* Reston, VA: National Association of Secondary School Principals. (ERIC Reproduction Service No. ED 240661)

Wexley, K. N., & Latham, G. P. (1982). *Developing and training human resources in organizations.* Glenview, IL: Scott, Foresman.

Wexley, K. N., & Yuki, G. A. (1984). *Organizational behavior and personnel psychology* (rev. ed.). Homewood, IL: Irwin.

Wiersma, W., & Gibney, T. (1985). Observation as an approach to measuring teacher competency. *Action in Teacher Education, 7,* 59-67.

Wise, A. E., & Darling-Hammond, L. (1985). Teacher evaluation and professionalism. *Educational Leadership, 42*(4), 28-33.

Wise, A. E., Darling-Hammond, L., McLaughlin, M., & Bernstein, H. T. (1984). *Teacher evaluation: A study of effective practices.* Santa Monica, CA: Rand.

FEEDBACK FORM

The Joint Committee, in an effort to obtain feedback on the *Standards*, has provided the feedback form on the next page for the reader's convenience. Detach and return the form for: (1) information regarding the review process for the *Standards*; (2) a supply of feedback and citation forms; and (3) directions regarding the use of the forms. Please refer to Invitation to Users for an overview of the plan for review and improving the *Standards*.

General inquiries concerning the *Standards* should be directed to:

Joint Committee on Standards for Education Evaluation
c/o The Evaluation Center
Western Michigan University
Kalamazoo, MI 49008-5178
(616) 387-5895

Please send review process information, a supply of feedback and citation forms, and directions for the use of the forms to:

———————————————————————————————————

Name

———————————————————————————————————

Institution

———————————————————————————————————

Address

———————————————————————————————————

———————————————————————————————————